Children & Other Wild Animals

✳

Other Books by Brian Doyle

fiction

The Plover

Mink River

Cat's Foot

Bin Laden's Bald Spot & Other Stories

poems

A Shimmer of Something

Thirsty for the Joy: Australian & American Voices

Epiphanies & Elegies

nonfiction

*The Grail: A Year Ambling & Shambling Through an
Oregon Vineyard in Pursuit of the Best Pinot Noir
in the Whole Wild World*

The Wet Engine: Exploring the Mad Wild Miracle of the Heart

essay collections

The Thorny Grace of It

Grace Notes

Leaping: Revelations & Epiphanies

Spirited Men

Saints Passionate & Peculiar

Credo

Two Voices (with Jim Doyle)

Children & Other Wild Animals

Notes on badgers, otters, sons, hawks, daughters, dogs,
bears, air, bobcats, fishers, mascots, Charles Darwin,
newts, sturgeon, roasting squirrels, parrots, elk, foxes,
tigers, and various other zoological matters

✳

Brian Doyle

Edited & with a Foreword by Cort Conley

Drawings by Mary Miller Doyle

Oregon State University Press
Corvallis

The paper in this book meets the guidelines for permanence and dura-
bility of the Committee on Production Guidelines for Book Longevity
of the Council on Library Resources and the minimum requirements of
the American National Standard for Permanence of Paper for Printed
Library Materials Z39.48-1984.

Excerpt from "Never to Have Loved a Child" from *Dusty Angels*
by Michael Blumenthal (BOA Editions, 1999). Used by permission.

Library of Congress Cataloging-in-Publication Data

Doyle, Brian.
   [Essays. Selections]
   Children and other wild animals : notes on badgers, otters, sons,
hawks, daughters, dogs, bears, air, bobcats, fishers, mascots, charles
darwin, newts, sturgeon, roasting squirrels, parrots, elk, foxes, tigers
and various other zoological matters / Brian Doyle.
      pages cm
   Summary: "Novelist and essayist Brian Doyle describes encounters
with astounding beings of every sort and shape in this collection of
short vignettes. The book gathers previously unpublished work along
with selections that have been published in *Orion, The Sun,* and *The
American Scholar,* among others."
— Provided by publisher.
   ISBN 978-0-87071-754-3 (paperback)
   1. Title.
   PR9199.3.D617A6 2014
   814'.54—dc23
                          2014031809

Oregon State University Press
121 The Valley Library
Corvallis OR 97331-4501
541-737-3166 • fax 541-737-3170
www.osupress.oregonstate.edu

To my brother Thomas More Patrick Doyle, with love.
No one knows more about fish and birds than that guy.

Contents

II. Brief Inquiries & Observances of the Wilder Animals We
Call Children for Lack of a Better Generic Label for Those
Most Headlong of Mammals; with Sidelong Glances at
Human Beings & the Seething Roaring
Natural World in Which We Swim

Foreword

A light year ago, or so it seems, my then-ten-year-old daughter regularly ensnared me in spirited wrangles about whether any detectable difference exists between animals and human beings—human beings being mammals, after all. I fumbled to defend my keystone species (*Homo sapiens* = wise man, no?) against her animal bias.

Conscience? I suggested. *Art? A soul, perhaps?*—only to discover that "animal" derives from the Latin *anima*, for soul, and that most of the world's religions and oldest cultures espouse, rather devoutly, a belief in an animal spirit or soul; at minimum, a partnership between animals and human animals, all being part of creation.

My daughter, unconvinced, straightaway became a vegan, and soon enough went in hot pursuit of a PhD in biology; ever after I have thought, What do I know about regard, equal and mutual, among all creatures?

Happily, however, Brian Doyle knows a good deal more about this regard, as the reader will readily learn; he is also a ringmaster of the familiar essay, "the most naked and direct and honest and playful and piercing form of all," as he says, "the closest to the speaking voice and the loose wandering penetrating free-associating story-junkie mind."

So if you picked up this book because its wry title and animated cover photo of the kid in a witness-protection program struck you as beguiling or provocative, congratulations—you are about to unearth a writer who is both mother lode and father lode, a lost-treasure mine in the literary landscape of the American West.

Doyle is a home-schooled naturalist who combines penetrating observation with kookaburra laughter every other page. Yet a general mansuetude flows through it all: his wild-world insights and sensibilities—unlike, for example, poet Robinson Jeffers' "I'd sooner, except the penalties, kill a man than a hawk"—embrace the sane *and* the humane. He knows beaver and otter, elk and wolf and sturgeon. Blue jay and chickadee. Children of all ages and species. Still, he ranks none above the others and condescends to none; all are to be witnessed, celebrated, and sung as the vibrant verbs and shards they are. His essays, taken all together, are finally about astonishment available in every moment and place; like the first time you saw neon tetra in a pet mart, such electric miracles in such a reeky cellblock.

Moreover, not to put too fine a point on it, as researchers discover that the songs, sounds, and rituals—the "language"—of birds, fish, and mammals actually rival in complexity human communication, then the link between child and dog grows ever more cousinly. Recent understandings, for instance, tell us that moths have memory; that ravens play like otters; that young rats like to be tickled; that chimps and cheetahs and elephants grieve. Like us. Just like us.

As for children, Doyle has turned fatherhood into an assisted triple play, a hat trick. And only a parent, I'm convinced, could have written these essays, informed by what he calls "the wild stimulus of our children." Children—parenthood in particular—are the brightest threads running through these pieces. As he says, "This is Being a Parent, and it's essentially impossible to explain or train for, and it makes you gaunt and gray, and the only tools that really help are patience and love and sleep, but o the joy." Elsewhere, he adds, "we used to *be* them, and we remember, dimly, what it was like to be small and frightened and confused."

In one of his more memorable poems, "Never to Have Loved a Child," Michael Blumenthal put it this way:

> *Never to have loved a child*
> *may be never to see again our pre-*
> *disillusionary selves, those faces*
> *gazing upward into the light, how innocent*
> *and beautiful and enraged they once were,*
> *and what has become of them now.*

This remarkable aggregation of essays is, of course, another child of Doyle's range, his memories (from napping as a kindergartner to the minefield cartwheels of a teenager), and his relentless observations. Lucky man, because as a fellow accomplished word-herder says, "stories only happen to people who can tell them." Tell them he surely can. His pencil never fails us.

For my part, after reading *Children & Other Wild Animals*, I came away thinking of Emily Dickinson lowering her basket from her second-story window with treats for children, and her last words: "Let us love better, children, it's most that's left to do."

—Cort Conley

Cort Conley is the literature director for the Idaho Commission on the Arts.

I.

Brief Disquisitions on Sturgeon, Foxes, Badgers, Trout, Mascots, Fishers, Bears, Squirrels, Dogs, Bobcats, Parrots, & the Bovine Population, Among Others of Our Astounding Neighbors

A Newt Note

One time, years ago, I was shuffling with my children through the vast wet moist dripping enormous thicketed webbed muddy epic forest on the Oregon coast, which is a forest from a million years ago, the forest that hatched the biggest creatures that ever lived on this bruised blessed earth, all due respect to California and its redwood trees but our cedars and firs made them redwoods look like toothpicks, and my kids and I were in a biggest-creature mood, because we had found slugs *way* longer than bananas, and footprints of elk that must have been gobbling steroids, and a friend had just told us of finding a bear print the size of a dinner plate, and all of us had seen whales in the sea that very morning, and all of us had seen pelicans too which look like flying pup tents, and how *do* they know to all hit cruise control at the same time, does the leader give a hand signal? as my son said, and one of us had seen the two ginormous young eagles who lived somewhere in this forest, so when we found the biggest stump in the history of the world, as my daughter called it, we were not exactly surprised, it was basically totally understandable that suddenly there would be a stump so enormous that it was like someone had dropped a dance floor into the forest, that's the sort of thing that *happens* in this forest, and my kids of course immediately leapt up on it and started shaking their groove thangs, and dancing themselves silly, and I was snorting with laughter until one kid, the goofiest, why we did not name this kid Goofy when we had the chance in those first few dewy minutes of life I will never know, well, this kid of course shimmed over to the edge and fell off head over teakettle, vanishing into a mat of fern nearly as tall as me, but the reason I tell you this story is that while we were all down in the moist velvet dark of the roots of the ferns, trying to be solicitious about Goofy and see if he was busted anywhere serious but also trying not to laugh and whisper the word *doofus,* one of us found a newt! o my god! Dad! check it *out!*

Of course the newt, rattled at the attention, peed on the kid who held it, and of course that led to screeching and hilarity, and of course on the way home we saw damselflies mating, which also led to screeching and hilarity, but the point of this story isn't pee or lust, however excellent a story about pee or lust would be. It's that one day when my kids and I were shuffling through the vast wet moist forest, we saw so many wonders and miracles that not one of us ever forgot any of the wonders and miracles we saw, and we saw tiny shreds and shards of the ones that are there, and what kind of greedy criminal thug thieves would we be as a people and a species if we didn't spend every iota of our cash and creativity to protect and preserve a world in which kids wander around gaping in wonder and hoping nothing else rubbery and astonishing will pee on them? You know what I mean?

In Otter Words

One day I am sitting in my old body at my old desk reading young essays, these are essays sent to me by holy children of various sizes, and I can feel the joy sloshing and rising in me as their words pour in, and finally I get topped off by the phrase *in otter words*, a child has scrawled this in the brightest green ink you ever saw, *in otter words, the holy parts are circled*, she writes. I think maybe the top of my head is going to fly off from happiness, and what remains of my organized mature mind sprints away giggling and mooing with pleasure. You know how it's said that human beings are the only beings who can contemplate two opposing ideas at once? It's even better than that—we can entertain *lots* of joyous ideas at the same time, it turns out. Such as, o my god, *otter words*, that's enough right there for hours of happy speculation, am I right? I mean, what *are* the otter words for trout and rain and minnows and ice and fur that has been warmed by the sun to just the right sheen and shimmer? I bet there *are* otter words for that, and for clumsy fishermen, and for osprey, and for mud of exactly the right consistency for sliding in, and for dying chinook salmon like ancient riddled kings, and old red drift boats, and young mergansers, and huge herons, and the basso murmur of mossy boulders grumbling at the bottom of the river, and the tinny querulous voices of crawdads, and the speed-freak chitter of chickadees, and the fat feet of tiny kids, and the little pebbly houses of caddisflies, and the rain of salmonflies in season like tiny orange helicopters. And *the holy parts!* which are *circled*, we knew that was true, the holy parts *are* underlined and il-luminated and highlighted, aren't they, and circled with a huge honking blessed magic marker, isn't that so? Sometimes I feel like the eyes in my heart close quietly without me paying much attention, and I muddle and mutter along thinking I am savoring and celebrating, and then *wham* a kid, it's always a kid, says something so piercing and wild and funny and unusual that *wham* my heart opens again like a door flung open by, say, an otter, and *wham*, I am completely and utterly overwhelmed and thrilled by the shocking brilliant uniform that kestrels wear, and moved beyond words by the roiling sea in a woman's eyes, and I get the shivering willies hearing my dad's gentle snortling laugh on the phone, and my *god* have you ever seen a blue jay up close and personal, what a cheerful arrogant street criminal it is, all blue brass and natty swagger, isn't that so? And most of all, best of all, better than every other joy and thrill, even the very best beer, which is a *very* excellent thing, are kids. Sure, they learn to lie, and sure, they are just not as into dental hygiene as you wish they were, and my *god* they skin their knees nine times a day, and do things like smear peanut butter on their abraded knees just to see what it feels like, and shake flour on the dog! so that when he shakes off the flour at one million revolutions per minute there will be a flour cloud in the kitchen the size of Utah!, isn't that *cool*, Dad?, but more than anything else in the world it is kids who make us see that the holy parts are circled. You know and I know this is true. We forget. I think maybe we should write it down somewhere, like on the wall by the coffeepot, or in steamy words on the bathroom mirror, so we will see it every day, and remember it more, and be refreshed to the bottom of our bony bottoms. If necessary use otter words.

Imagining Foxes

One time, many years ago, when the world and I were young, I spent a day in a tiny cedar forest with my sister and brother. This was in the marshlands of an island the first people there called Paumonok. This little cedar forest was twelve city blocks long by two blocks wide, for a total of 84 acres, and there was a roaring highway at the northern end, and a seriously busy artery road at the southern end, but when you were in Tackapausha Preserve you were, no kidding, deep in the woods, and you couldn't hear cars and sirens and radios no matter how hard you tried. We tried hard, my kid brother and I, we sat silently for probably the longest time we ever had, up to that point, but our sister was right, and we *were* deep in the wild.

We saw woodpeckers and an owl and *lots* of warblers—this was spring, and there were more warblers than there were taxicabs on Fifth Avenue. We saw what we thought was a possum but which may have been a squirrel with a glandular problem. We saw muskrats in the two little ponds. We saw a hummingbird, or one of us *said* he saw a hummingbird, but this was the brother who claimed that saints and angels talked to him in the attic, so I am not sure we saw a hummingbird, technically. We did not see deer, although we did see mats of grass which sure looked like places where deer would nap like uncles after big meals, sprawled on their sides with their vests unbuttoned, snoring like heroes. We saw holes among the roots of the white cedars which were so clearly the dens of animals like foxes and weasels and badgers that one of us looked for mail addressed to them outside their doors. We saw scratch marks in the bark of trees that one of us was sure were made by bears although our sister said she was not sure there were bears registered in the Seaford School District, not to mention badgers either.

We saw many other amazing small things that are not small, and we wandered so thoroughly and so energetically all afternoon, that my kid brother and I slept all the way home in the back seat of the car with our mouths hanging open like trout or puppies, sleeping so soundly that we both drooled on the naugahyde seat and our sister had to mop up after us with the beach towel she always carried in the trunk for just such droolery, but my point here is not what we saw, or even the excellence of gentle patient generous older sisters; it's about what we did not see. We did not see a fox. I can assure you we did not see a fox. I could trot out my brother and sister today to testify that we did not see a fox. With all my mature and adult and reasonable and sensible old heart I bet there were zero foxes then resident in Tackapausha Preserve, between Sunrise Highway and Merrick Road, in the county of Nassau, in the great state of New York. But I tell you we *smelled* Old Reynard, his scent of old blood and new honey, and we heard his sharp cough and bark, and if you looked just right you could see his wry paw prints in the dust by his den, and if we never take our kids to the little strips of forests, the tiny shards of beaches, the ragged forgotten corner thickets with beer bottles glinting in the duff, they'll never even *imagine* a fox, and what kind of world is that, where kids don't imagine foxes? We spend so much time mourning and battling for a world where kids can *see* foxes that we forget you don't have to see foxes. You have to imagine them, though. If you stop imagining them then they are all dead, and what kind of world is that, where all the foxes are dead?

Fishering

In the woods here in Oregon there is a creature that eats squirrels like candy, can kill a pursuing dog in less than a second, and is in the habit of deftly flipping over porcupines and scooping out the meat as if the prickle-pig was a huge and startled breakfast melon. This riveting creature is the fisher, a member of the mustelid family that includes weasels, otter, mink, badgers, ferrets, marten, and (at the biggest and most ferocious end of the family) wolverine. Sometimes called the pekan or fisher-cat, the fisher can be three feet long (with tail) and weigh as much as twelve pounds. Despite its stunning speed and agility, it is best known not as an extraordinary athlete of the thick woods and snowfields but as the bearer of a coat so dense and lustrous that it has been sought eagerly by trappers for thousands of years; which is one reason the fisher is so scarce pretty much everywhere it used to live.

Biologist friends of mine tell me there are only two "significant" populations of fisher in Oregon — one in the Siskiyou Mountains in the southwest, called the Klamath population, and the other in the Cascade Mountains south of Crater Lake, called the Cascade population. All of the rare sightings of fisher in Oregon in recent years have been in these two areas. In the northwest coastal woods where I occasionally wander, biologists tell me firmly, there are no fishers and there have been none for more than fifty years.

I am a guy who wanders around looking for nothing in particular, which is to say everything; in this frame of mind I have seen many things, in many venues urban and suburban and rural, and while ambling in the woods I have seen marten kits and three-legged elk and secret beds of watercress and the subtle dens of foxes. I have found thickets of wild grapevines, and secret jungles of salmonberries, and stands of huckleberries so remote and so delicious that it is a moral dilemma for me as to whether or not I should leave a map behind for my children when the time comes for me to add to the compost of the world.

Suffice it to say that I have been much graced in these woods, but to see a fisher was not a gift I expected. Yet recently I found loose quills on the path and then the late owner of the quills, with his or her conqueror atop the carcass staring at me.

I do not know if the fisher had ever seen a human being before; it evinced none of the usual sensible caution of the wild creature confronted with *homo violencia*, and it showed no inclination whatsoever to retreat from its prize. We stared at each other for a long moment and then I sat down, thinking that a reduction of my height and a gesture of repose might send the signal that I was not dangerous and had no particular interest in porcupine meat. Plus I remembered that a fisher can slash a throat in less than a second.

Long minutes passed. The fisher fed, cautiously. I heard thrushes and wrens. There were no photographs or recordings and when the fisher decided to evanesce I did not make casts of its tracks or claim the former porcupine as evidence of fisherness. I just watched and listened and now I tell you. I don't have any heavy message to share. I was only a witness: where there are no fishers there was a fisher. It was a stunning creature, alert, attentive, accomplished, unafraid. I think maybe there is much where we think there is nothing. Where there are no fishers there was a fisher. Remember that.

Walking the Pup

First we go by the place where one time there was a squashed squirrel she rolled in, because you never know, there might be something newly dead to roll in, and then we go *way* around the bush where she got stung by a bee, and then we go by the new house with the shrill tiny psychopathic dog whom we studiously ignore, which drives it insane, which makes us unaccountably happy, and then we go past the dark house where the brooding evil cat lives who looks eerily like Marge Schott, former owner of the Cincinnati Reds baseball team, the wild hair and bad language and cigarette reek and everything, and the cat snarls at us as usual, and the pup makes that yearning sound in her throat that means *please let me eat the cat* and I say *someday, my pretty* in the Wicked Witch voice, and we keep moving on down the road.

We go past the place where sometimes the jays hang out like a little blue biker gang, and past the blackberry brambles where one time there was a rabbit! and the pup took off like a racehorse! and I thought it was spinal surgery for me for sure!, and we come to the busy street where I always make her pause and idle and look both ways, even if there are no cars, and I say quietly *dog, there will come a day when you will thank me for this lesson*, and she hoists her ears to indicate that she is pretending that I have said something interesting, and we resume our voyage.

Up the street there is the drain where you can always hear water rushing madly down to the river even on the driest hottest days, and we stop and listen for a while, because burbling hurrying headlong water is a cool sound, and then we go by the big telephone pole where all dogs leave messages, and then we go by the tree where one time we saw a sharp-shinned hawk *almost* catch a crow, *that* was a great day, and then we go behind the bagel store and sniff around for old bagels, and then we go by the coffee shop where the owner leaves a bowl of water for dogs wandering by, and then we check behind the pizza shop just in case, and then we head home through the tiny park that used to be an orchard, where now there are always baseballs and tennis balls and crows and cookies and sneakers and worms and crickets and other good things to eat, and then we stop at the creek for a guzzle, and usually right about there one of us pees like a racehorse, and then we come back downhill through the woods where the hope springs eternal in both of us that there might be a deer or an elk or a bear.

One time when we were walking through those woods I told her that me personally myself I thought it would be pretty cool to someday encounter a wolverine in these woods, but that this seemed unlikely, as there just aren't as many wolverine around as there used to be, although it seems to me that you can never be totally sure you *won't* meet a wolverine, because just last year as scientists were saying with absolute conviction that wolverine were absolutely incontrovertibly extinct here, a woman ran over a wolverine on the highway, which seems like pretty much a confirmed sighting of a wolverine to me. Although the thing is that while the papers were then filled with learned commentary about mustelid populations and restoration of native species and all, I kept thinking about the woman limping her dented car home and her husband asks *what happened to the car?* and she answers *I hit a wolverine,* which is a phrase you hardly ever hear.

While I was telling her this story the pup looked at me like maybe I was saying something interesting, but I have since concluded that what she was thinking is that a dead wolverine would be something *really* cool to roll in, which I guess it would be, if you like that sort of thing, which I do not, though I will defend *your* right to roll in deceased members of the mustelid family, this being a free country and all, which is cooler even than rolling in what used to be a wolverine, you know what I mean?

Twenty Things the Dog Ate

1. Ancient squashed dried round flat shard of beaver
Sweet mother of the mewling baby Jesus! You wouldn't think a creature that likes to watch Peter O'Toole movies would be such an omnivorous gobbling machine, but he has eaten everything from wasps to the back half of a raccoon. But let us not ignore the beaver. Speculation is that beaver was washed up onto road when the overflowing lake blew its dam, was squashed by a truck, and then got flattened ten thousand times more, and then summer dried it out hard and flat as a manhole cover, and the dog somehow pried it up, leaving only beaver oil on the road, and *ate it*. Sure, he barfed later. Wouldn't you?

2. Young sparrow
I kid you not. Sparrow falls from nest in the pine by the fence, flutters down ungainly to unmerciful earth, dog leaps off porch like large hairy mutant arrow, gawps bird in half an instant. Man on porch roars *drop it!* Dog emits bird with a choking coughing sound, as if disgusted by a misplaced apostrophe. Bird staggers for a moment and then flutters awkwardly up to fencepost. I wouldn't have believed this if I had not seen it with my own holy eyeballs. Wonder how fledgling bird explained *that* adventure to mom.

3. Crayons
I don't even want to think about this ever again. Crayola. The big box—sixty-four crayons, all colors. Sure, he barfed later. Sure he did. Wouldn't you?

4. Yellowjacket wasps
Every summer. Even though he gets stung again and again
in the nether reaches of his mouth and throat, and jumps up
whirling around in such a manner that we laugh so hard we
have to pee. He cannot resist snapping them out of the air as
if they were bright bits of candy, and then whirling around
making high plaintive sounds like a country singer on laughing
gas. I have to pee.

5. Jellyfish on the shore of the vast and impacific Pacific
Why would you ever do such a thing? What could possibly look
less appetizing than an oozing quivering deceased jellyfish? Yet
he does. Sure, he barfs.

6. to 19. Some non-organic highlights
Pencil nubs. Lacrosse balls. The cricket ball a friend sent me
from Australia. Pennies. Postcards. Sports sections. Bathrobe
belts. Kindling sticks. Kazoos. Most of a paperback copy of
Harry Potter and the Order of the Phoenix. Most of a cell-phone
charger. Pen caps. Toothbrushes. One of two tiny sneakers that
belonged to a child one month old, although to be fair there it
wasn't like the kid was actually *using* the sneakers.

20. An entire red squirrel, called a chickaree in these parts
I think the squirrel was suicidal. If *you* were a squirrel the size
of a banana, and *you* could evade a dog with the athletic gifts
and predatory instinct of Michael Jordan, would *you* venture
down to the grass for any reason whatsoever, knowing that the
dog could change you from present to past tense in less than
a second? Would you? Me neither. But the squirrel did. The

skull appeared magically in the grass two days later. The Dog declined to eat the skull a second time, probably for religious reasons. After a while a crow carried it off, probably for religious reasons. One of the great things about our country, I think, is the range of religions here, each one odder than all the rest.

A Note on Mascots

The first sports team I remember loving as a child, in the dim dewy days when I was two or three years old and just waking up to things that were not milk and mama and dirt and dogs, was the Fighting Irish of the University of Notre Dame, who were on television every day, it seemed, in our bustling brick Irish Catholic house; and then, inasmuch as I was hatched and coddled near Manhattan, there were Metropolitans and Knickerbockers and Rangers and Islanders; and then, as I shuffled shyly into high school, there were, for the first time, snarling and roaring mammalian mascots, notably the Cougars of my own alma mater, which was plopped in marshlands where I doubt a cougar had been seen for three hundred years; but right about then I started paying attention to how we fetishize animals as symbols for our athletic adventures, and I have become only more attentive since, for I have spent nearly thirty years now working for colleges and universities, and you could earn a degree in zoology just by reading the college sports news, where roar and fly and sprint and lope and canter and gallop and prowl animals from anteater to wasp—among them, interestingly, armadillos, bees, boll weevils, herons, owls, koalas, turtles, moose, penguins, gulls, sea lions, and squirrels, none of which seem especially intimidating or prepossessing, although I know a man in North Carolina who once lost a fistfight with a heron, and certainly many of us have run away from angry bees and moose, and surely there are some among us who could relate stories of furious boll weevils, but perhaps this is not the time, although anyone who *has* a story like that should see me right after class.

There are vast numbers of canids (coyotes, foxes, huskies, salukis, wolves), felids (lions, tigers, panthers, lynx, bobcats), ruminants (bulls, chargers, broncs, broncos, and bronchoes, though no bronchials), mustelids (badgers, wolverine, otters), and denizens of the deep (dolphins, gators, sharks, sailfish, and "seawolves," or orca). There are two colleges which have an aggrieved camel as their mascot. There are schools represented by snakes and tomcats. There is a school whose symbol is a frog and one whose mascot is a large clam and one whose mascot famously is a slug. There is a school whose mascot is the black fly. There are the Fighting Turtles of the College of Insurance in New York. There are schools represented by lemmings and scorpions and spiders. There are the Fighting Stormy Petrels of Oglethorpe University in Georgia. There is a school represented by an animal that has never yet been seen in the Americas, the bearcat of Asia, although perhaps that is meant to be a wolverine, which did once inhabit southern Ohio, and may still live in Cincinnati, which has tough neighborhoods. The most popular mascot appears to be the eagle, especially if you count the fifteen schools represented by golden eagles, which brings us to a round total of eighty-two schools symbolized by a bird Benjamin Franklin considered "a bird of bad moral character, too lazy to fish for himself ... like those among men who live by sharping & robbing he is generally poor and often very lousy. Besides he is a rank coward ..." But the two schools that Franklin helped establish are nicknamed the Quakers and the Diplomats, so we can safely ignore Ben on this matter.

And this is not even to delve into the mysterious world of fantastical fauna—blue bears and blue tigers, crimson hawks, trolls, dragons and firebirds, griffins and griffons and gryphons, delta devils and jersey devils (there are a *lot* of devils, which says something interesting), jayhawks and kohawks and duhawks, green eagles and phoenixes, thunderhawks and thunderwolves, the mind reels, and then there is the whole subset of nicknamery that has to do with botany, as evidenced most memorably by the Fighting Violets of New York University, on which image we had better pull this whole essay to the side of the road and sit silently for a moment.

Beyond all the obvious reasons we choose animals as symbols for our sporting teams—their incredible energy and muscle, grace and strength, intelligence and verve, our ancient conviction of their power and magic, ancient associations as clan signs and tribal totems, even more ancient shivers perhaps of fear at animals who hunted and ate us, not to mention the way their images look cool on letterhead and sweatshirts and pennants and fundraising appeals—there is something else, something so deep and revelatory about human beings that I think we do not admit it because it is too sad. I think we love animals as images because we miss them in the flesh, and I think we love them as images because they matter to us spiritually in ways we cannot hope to articulate. The vast majority of us will never see a cougar or a wolverine, not to mention a boll weevil, but even wearing one on a shirt, or shouting the miracle of its name in a stadium, or grinning to see its rippling beauty on the window of a car, gives us a tiny subtle crucial electric jolt in the heart, connects us somehow to what we used to be with animals, which was thrilled and terrified. We've lost the salt of that feeling forever, but even a hint of it matters immensely to us as animals too. Maybe that's what we miss the most—the feeling that they are our cousins, and not clans of creatures who once filled the earth and now are shreds of memory, mere symbols, beings who used to be.

The Unspoken Language of the Eyes

A man named Nicholas tells me that yes, he did find a stunned bobcat on the road as he came home from work, this was near the Lucky River here in Oregon, and something made me stop, he says, I thought, *my gawd that's a wildcat!* and it's not like you see a bobcat sprawled in the road every day, you know, so I stop to see if it's dead, but I see he's breathing but unconscious, so I pick him up. He weighed about what a toddler weighs. He was amazingly beautiful. You wouldn't believe the intense softness of his fur. And the colors of his fur ... I don't have the right words for the colors. I put him on the floorboard in the front, on the passenger side. I have a Honda Prelude. He was bleeding from the eyes and nose and mouth. In my head and perhaps out loud I spoke to him a bit, and I am absolutely sure he heard me, at some level. He was unconscious but aware, you know what I mean? I was being respectful, telling him what I was doing, that I was getting him help, asking politely that he not rip my face off if he woke up startled to find himself in a Honda Prelude. We drove about twenty minutes. I got all the way into town and was looking for the vet, when he woke up. He sort of stretched and then snapped to his feet, growling. I pulled over. We were on Fourth Street. I raised my right hand slowly and started talking. We kept our eyes on each other. I kept my hand up. I just wanted us to sink into a calm space, you know? People keep asking what I *said* to him but I just talked in a calm even tone. I don't remember quite what I said. People think it's comical, a man talking to a bobcat, or insane, I mean a bobcat is a serious carnivore with razors for claws, but there was an awareness between us, an intense presence, a recognition of intention, that is very hard to explain and was the most extraordinary thing. It was dark by now but there was enough light in the car to see by. He had green eyes. I kept talking in a calm even voice and we kept staring at each other. There were some moments of silence also. I cannot explain how genuine and sincere this was. It was a life very present with another life for a little while. There was a mutual understanding of no harm. We sat there for a while and then I slowly brought my hand down and put the emergency brake on. I kept on talking and we kept our attention on each other. He had white tufts of fur on his ears. After a while I opened my door and slowly got out of the car. He remained calm. I walked around the car. We kept our eyes on each other. Eventually all the rest of it happened, Jeff from the Chintimini Wildlife Rehabilitation Center got him out of the car with a noose, as gently as he could, and the cat was *not* happy about the noose, there's fur and feces all over the car, but he's fine now, he had two broken teeth which were fixed and he's recovering and will be released back into the woods next week. He's three years old. The paper here ran a story, which was picked up by the wire services, and a television crew came and all that, but no one told the story right. The real story is the unspoken language of the eyes. The real story is the intensity of awareness between two creatures. Some people don't get it. Like one guy who said the bobcat would look great on his wall. He doesn't get it. This is a *stunning* creature. For a few minutes there we were totally aware of each other, complete and utter attention, with an unspoken understanding of no harm, and some kind of what you might call, if you were thrashing around for words that don't fit very well but they're the only words you can find, a sort of spiritual connection.

That was ... I don't have the right words. Amazing, riveting, moving, genuine. Could you try to tell this story in a way that focuses on what was the most amazing thing, that intensity of presence? *That's* the story.

The Bishop's Parrot

Bishop Charles O'Reilly, the first Catholic bishop of Baker, Oregon, was occasionally astride a horse, and Bishop Leo Fahey, also of Baker, was often astride a horse, and Bishop Thomas Connolly, also of Baker, was *always* on a horse, except when he was telling stories like the one about a bishop and a cougar and an owl in a cave, but my favorite story about bishops and animals, except for the story of Archbishop Edward Howard, of Portland, wrestling a sturgeon in his native Iowa, is the story of the late Bishop Paul Waldschmidt, of Portland, and his beloved parrot Kuzuku, of whom there are many stories, like the one of Kuzuku outlining ideas for sermons to the bishop, who liked to tell that story himself, to the general astonishment of the faithful. There are even more stories about the Bishop than there are about Kuzuku; for example the story of then-merely-Father Paul, in seminary in Maryland, being required to make a trip into the wilderness, for some lost spiritual or character-building reason, and Father Paul, being something of a gourmand even then, setting off with buckets of champagne and huge steaks strapped to the sides of burly mules, while he rode astride a horse the size of Utah; interestingly the only story that I know in which he appears with a horse.

But we were talking of the parrot, which was famously ill-tempered with people other than the bishop, which is the reverse of the bishop's approach to life, Paul being the soul of cheerful courtesy to all and sundry, even those who mistook him for a gardener at the university where he was president before his elevation to the bishop's chair, an understandable mistake, considering that you could often find Paul in a vast pair of overalls, grubbing in his beloved rock garden high above the river, in the hours when he was not saving the university from extinction, or happily eating sausages and drinking beer with his students, not a habit many presidents maintain today, which is too bad.

But of mutual projects other than sermons between parrot and bishop we know little, which is a shame. Could it not be that they were writing a novel together? Perhaps they were both past masters of chess, or the spinning of silk into prayer scarves? Could it be that they read the works of Washington Irving to each other at night, taking great pleasure in the slightly stilted prose? Or perhaps they both detested Ayn Rand and took a devious glee in explicating her essentially fascist stance, her wooden characters, and her worship of the ego as the only divinity? Or perhaps they were serious students of the ancient Roman Republic and meticulous scholars of the machinations of the Caesars as that Republic morphed sadly into mere dictatorships, each bloodier than the last, until finally they were no more, and what arose as a brave amalgam of hill villages over the Tiber faded into the dusty pages of books?

This could be; but Kuzuku no longer speaks since the death of the bishop, and it may be that the loss of his friend is a daily shock to him, a hole that will not heal. It may be that parrots have bigger hearts than we know. It may be that every creature alive is wilder with love than we know. It may be that the genius of that for which we have no words, that which set the stars to burn, was to give us hearts wilder than we ever imagined. It may be that an aged parrot, living silently with tiny nuns who carry him on their shoulders to the chapel every evening to pray, dreams nightly of a world made utterly wild with love; perhaps that is what he and the bishop dreamed together, in their evenings by the fire; perhaps that is what we will dream now, here at the end of the world we did not love enough, the world still wild for us.

The Creature Beyond the Mountains

There are fish in the rivers of Cascadia that are bigger and heavier than your car. To haul the biggest ones out of the Columbia River fishermen once used horses and oxen. These creatures are so enormous and so protected by bony armor and so averse to biting or eating people that no one picks on them, so they grow to be more than a hundred years old, maybe two hundred years old; no one knows. Sometimes in winter they gather in immense roiling balls in the river, maybe for heat, maybe for town meetings, maybe for wild sex; no one knows. A ball of more than sixty thousand of them last year rolled up against the bottom of a dam in the Columbia, causing a nervous United States Army Corps of Engineers to send a small submarine down to check on the dam. They eat fish, clams, rocks, fishing reels, shoes, snails, beer bottles, lamprey, eggs, insects, fishing lures, cannonballs, cats, ducks, crabs, basketballs, squirrels, and many younger members of their species; essentially they eat whatever they want. People have fished for them using whole chickens as bait, with hooks the size of your hand. They like to follow motorboats, for reasons no one knows. As with human beings, the males wish to spawn in their early teens, but the females wait until their twenties. The females then produce epic rafts of eggs, three or four million at a time, from ovaries than can weigh more than two hundred pounds. On average three of those eggs will grow to be mature fish. Some of the fish that have been caught have been fifteen feet long and weighed fifteen hundred pounds. There are documented stories and photographs of fish more than twenty feet long and two thousand pounds. A fish that long would be as tall as three Shaquille O'Neals and heavier than six. There is

a persistent legend in southwest Washington State that somewhere in a lake or pond near Mount Saint Helens is the biggest
fish of this kind that anyone has ever seen or heard about or
imagined, a fish so big that when it surfaces occasionally it is
mistaken for a whale, but this is the same region of the wild
and wondrous world where Sasquatch is thought to most likely
live, so you wonder.

The being of which we speak is *Acipenser transmontanus*,
the sturgeon beyond the mountains, popularly called the white
sturgeon, although it is not white, but as gray as the moist
lands in which it lives, the temperate rain forest west of the
Pacific mountains and east of the not-very-pacific ocean. From
northern Mexico to southern Alaska it cruises in the nether
reaches of rivers, battling only the sea lions that in recent years
have taken up residence in the coastal rivers of the west to
dine on salmon and young sturgeon, but I am sure there will
come a day when I will pick up my newspaper and read about
a precipitous decline in sea lion pups, and I will remember that
a new lion pup is not much bigger than a chicken or a cat or a
basketball, and I will conclude that *Acipenser transmontanus*
has exacted vengeance on sea lions by discovering yet another
cool new thing to eat, after a hundred million years of discovering new things to eat at the bottom of vast huge rivers. Taking
the long view, you have to admire the individual sturgeons,
very probably adolescent males, who over the years were the
first to eat such things as cats and cannon balls. Perhaps it
was accidental, they were on regular hoover patrol and were
just slurping up whatever wasn't finning away fast and furious, but perhaps not, perhaps it was a brave leap, and among
the sturgeon of today there are legends of the first heroes who
inhaled volleyballs and badgers. It could be.

*

At the Sturgeon Viewing and Interpretive Center, at the Bonneville Fish Hatchery, in Cascade Locks, Oregon, where Tanner Creek empties into the Columbia River, near the immense Bonneville Dam, there are three enormous sturgeon in a large open pond. Two of them, each about eight feet long and weighing about an eighth of a ton, have not as yet been given names by human beings. The third is Herman, the most famous sturgeon in Oregon. Herman is about eleven feet long and weighs perhaps six hundred pounds. No one knows how old he is. He might be ninety years old. There are references to Herman the Sturgeon in hatchery records beginning in 1925. It is thought that there have been several Hermans, some exhibited annually at the Oregon State Fair. This Herman, who is probably not the 1925 Herman, arrived at Bonneville twelve years ago, a mere nine feet and four hundred pounds, then. Many thousands of people come to see Herman every year, as they visit the hatchery's spawning rooms, holding ponds, rearing ponds, and egg incubation building, all of which are for salmon and steelhead; the three sturgeon here, and the pool of massive rainbow trout, are show ponies only, sturgeon and trout not being as close to extinction as salmon and steelhead. This hatchery alone raises a million coho salmon, eight million chinook, and three hundred thousand steelhead every year, for release into various Oregon rivers. There are fish everywhere at the hatchery, leaping and milling and swirling and startling visitors, and it is remarkable and amazing and moving to see so many miracles at once, so many mysterious beings, so many individual adventures, so much excellent flaky accompaniment to pinot noir, and to think where they will go and what they will see, some of them headed into the deepest thickets of the ocean, others into the bellies of animals of every size and shape, but pretty much every human visitor is here also to see Herman, and I station myself in a dark corner of the center one afternoon and view the human beings who come to view Herman.

There are nuns. There are schoolchildren. There is a man wearing a cat on his shoulder. There is a woman wearing not much more than a smile. There is a woman wearing white plastic thigh boots and a baseball jacket. There is a deputy mayor. There is a long-haul truck driver smoking a cigar that smells like something died in his truck in Ohio. There are teenagers holding hands. There is a man dressed head to toe in Seattle Seahawks fan gear, including sneakers on which he has written the number 8, for the star quarterback. There is a man with a cane and a woman with a walker. There is a girl in a wheelchair. There are tour groups, family outings, and a man wearing tuxedo trousers and gleaming black shoes and a motorcycle gang jacket. People eat and drink and joke and curse and smoke and spit and gape and dawdle and laugh and several ask me where's Herman? I say I am a mere onlooker as well and my experience is that he will hove into view after a while. Some people don't wait. Some people express annoyance with the hatchery management and the lack of organization as regards Herman's appearance. Others mistake Herman's eight-foot-long companions for Herman. Others wait silently for Herman to hove into view.

The most memorable viewing for me that day was a young man with a small boy who appeared to be his son. The father looked like he was about nineteen, with the wispy first mustache and chin-armpit of a teenager. The boy, wearing a red cowboy hat, seemed to be about three years old. The father tried to line the boy up for a photograph, tried to get the kid to stand still until Herman hove into view, but the boy skittered here and there like a rabbit, the father alternately wheedling and barking at him, and finally the boy stood still, but facing the wrong direction, with his nose pressed against the glass, and the father sighed and brought his camera down to his waist at exactly the moment that Herman slowly filled the window like a zeppelin. The boy leapt away from the window and his hat fell off. No one said a word. Herman kept sliding past for a long time. Finally his tail exited stage left and the boy said, awed, clear as a bell, *holy shit, Dad!* The father didn't say anything and they stood there another couple of minutes, both of them speechless, staring at where Herman used to be, and then they walked up the stairs holding hands.

On the way home to Portland, as I kept an eye out for osprey along the banks of the Columbia, I thought of that boy's face as Herman slid endlessly past the window. It's hilarious what he said, it's a great story, I'll tell it happily for years, but what lingers now for me is his utter naked amazement. He saw ancientness up close and personal. He saw a being he never dreamed was alive on this planet, a being he never imagined, a being beyond vast, a being that rendered him speechless with awe until he could articulate a raw blunt astonishment that you have to admire for its salty honesty. He saw wonder, face to face. Maybe wonder is the way for us with animals in the years to come. Maybe wonder is the way past the last million years of combat and into the next million years of something other than combat. Maybe the look on that kid's face is the face of the future.

*

The woman who married me, a slight mysterious riveting being not half as tall as Herman, grabs me by the beard in the kitchen one day and says *What is up with you and sturgeon, why are you so fascinated with sturgeon?* And I spend days afterwards trying to answer these questions for myself.

Part of it is bigness. The fact that there are wild creatures way bigger and heavier than cars *right there in the river, in a city of two million,* is astounding, and it is also astounding that everyone totally takes this for granted, whereas I would very much like to stop people in the street about this matter, and blast-text *OMG!!!,* and set up a continual river bottom video feed into all grade schools so kids everywhere in my state will quietly mutter *holy shit, Dad,* and establish the website MassiveSturgeonVisitation.com, so when a creature the size of a kindergarten bus slides to the surface suddenly in front of a Cub Scout dabbing for crab in the Columbia, he, the Cub Scout, can post an alert as soon as he changes his underwear. And the bigness of sturgeon here is mysteriously stitched, for me, into the character and zest and possibility of Cascadia; there are huge things here, trees and fish and mountains and rivers and personalities and energies and ideas, and somehow the pairing of power and peace in the piscatorial is a hint of the possible in people.

Part of it is harmlessness; they don't eat us, no matter how often we eat them. Adult sturgeon do not even have teeth, having dropped their weapons after gnashing through adolescence. We have a fairly straightforward relationship with most animals: we kill the ones who eat us, and we eat the rest. Most of the ones who eat us are bigger than we are—crocodiles, tigers, sharks, bears—but there are some animals that are bigger than we are that don't eat us, and at those we gape, and grope for some other emotion beyond paranoia and palate and pet. Whales, for example. We yearn for something *with* enormous gentle animals, something more than mammalian fellowship. We want some new friendship, some sort of intimate feeling, for which we don't have good words yet.

Part of it is sheer goofy wonder; I suppose to me sturgeon are a lovely example of all the zillions of things we do not know, for all our brilliance and inventiveness and cockiness, all our seeming confidence that we run the world. Most of what we know is that we don't know hardly anything, which cheers me up wonderfully. The world is still stuffed with astonishments beyond our wildest imagining—isn't that the most alluring sentence *ever*? Isn't that the sentence we should have pinned up on every bathroom mirror in the world, so we all see it first thing in the morning every blessed day before we brush our extant choppers?

Part of it is freshwaterness; the ocean is the densest wilderness on the planet, the jungle, the unexplored deep, filled with mysteries and monsters, mostly unmapped, the endless blue world where human beings are unmoored; whereas rivers are land veins, serpentine lakes, people paths, arteries through the muscled earth; and we are more comfortable in general with fresh water, which we drink and in which we bathe, than with salt, which we cannot drink and in which we are not only uncomfortable but essentially unwelcome. Even the biggest rivers and lakes are stories with endings, they can be plumbed, they are the land's liquid cousins, the land embraces them; whereas the ocean is landless, endless, wilderness, its denizens often savage and terrifying. So to ponder an enormous creature that is not terrifying, that lives in the river I can see from my office window, that remains pretty much a total mystery to biologists and ichthyologists and the United States Army Corps of Engineers—this gives me hope.

*

I ask fisherfolk what it's like to haul up a big sturgeon from the bottom of a river. Like dragging a refrigerator, says one man. Like fishing for bear, says another. Like having an air-conditioner on the end of your line and if you give it slack it will sink and if you pull too hard you will snap your line, so basically you are doomed to an hour's weightlifting, at the end of which you haul up a freaking nightmare from the Paleozoic, says another. Like having a couch on your line, says another. Like you hooked the whole bottom of the river and you will be there until the Cubs win the World Series, says another. Like you got a Chevy on your line, says another.

Do they fight when they feel the hook? I ask.

The little ones do, the ones up to five feet or so, says one man. The big ones, they basically say screw you. They basically say show me, bub. They don't seem real bothered by the hook. They take it real gentle, you know. They don't hammer your line. I think after a while they get bored and let you haul them up just so they can see what's going on at the surface. Mostly what's going on when you have hauled a big sturgeon up to the boat is that now you have a hernia. Your shoulders are shot for a month. And there's none of this thrill kill, like with a big salmon. A salmon looks like a *fish* fish. A sturgeon, you haul it up, it looks like your drunk uncle. It's like you fought and kicked and pulled and battled and then up comes Yoda on steroids. I seen people scream the first time they see one up close. One time I seen a guy haul one up and look all over puzzled for its mouth and when he found it he threw the fish back in real fast. I laughed so hard that time I thought I was going to pee my pants. Another time a guy caught a big one and brought it in and a kid on the dock saw it and ran like hell. That still makes me laugh. I bet that kid is still running. You should of seen that kid run. You know how someone runs when they are not thinking how they *look* when they run but they just want to be in the next county in like the next six seconds? That's how *that* kid ran. That still makes me laugh. *There's* a kid when someday in a restaurant he sees sturgeon on the menu he will have a fit, I bet. Now you got me laughing so hard I think I sprained my brain.

They have the most subtle bite, says a man who guides men and women to sturgeon in the mouth of the Mighty Columbia. We call it a soft bite. You're hardly aware your hook's been taken until you set and pull and realize there's a friggin' dinosaur on your line. And they're *very* fast. People don't think they are quick because they get so big. People think they are like manatees or whatever, but I seen them rip off fifty yards of line in ten seconds. They *dart*, man. Something to see, a ten-foot animal *whipping* through the water, and they jump like tarpon, and they tail-walk, especially in shallow water, and the first time you hook a serious dinosaur and he or she decides to light out for the territory you're ... flabbergasted. Awed. Fascinating animal. Very, very adaptable. They live deep, they live shallow, they eat everything, their only enemies are sea lions and us. What else can I tell you? They have the worst eyesight imaginable, but they have a *very* sharp sense of smell. You know what fascinates me the most, though? We don't know hardly anything about their lives. One sturgeon tagged in the Columbia showed up in San Francisco Bay. Others go out in the ocean and disappear for years. No one knows what they're doing or how far they travel. Isn't that cool? Funniest line I heard about sturgeon? I was fishing in the deep water by the Bonneville Dam once with a friend and a ten-foot sturgeon jumped out of the river suddenly about thirty yards away and my friend went pale and said *I will never, and I mean never, swim in this river again.* Boy, did that make me laugh. You should have seen his face. He was dead serious, too. I don't think he ever actually has been in the river since, no.

*

Sometimes for reasons no one knows sturgeon will suddenly rocket to the surface and fly out of the water and sail temporarily through the other ether. There are any number of theories about this: they are trying to dislodge parasites, they are exchanging water for air to escape predation, they are showing off for girls, they have totally lost their marbles, they are gunning for insects, they are communicating with other sturgeon in the river using terrific splashes as sonic flags, they are imitating trout and salmon, they are *teasing* trout and salmon, they are enduring digestive distress and wish to rearrange their contents, or they like to fly, briefly. Maybe every sturgeon deep in his or her heart wants to be an osprey. No one knows. This last explanation appeals to me, because I believe the sudden nutty urge to do something that doesn't make much sense is endemic to all living creatures, and is probably the reason evolution does indeed slowly shuffle forward, like Darwin in his garden looking for worms, because individual members of species do ridiculous things, against the disapproving mutter of society, and so discover flight and beer and the Hawaiian Islands, but it's also appealing to think that maybe sturgeon have a devious sense of humor, and they like to goof on salmon, and every once in a while a sturgeon will streak to the surface and explode aloft, saying to his posse, *hey look, I'm a chinook!* and all the sturgeon snigger rudely as the salmon glare and continue their commute, trying to maintain a silvery dignity, while ignoring the catcalls, so to speak, of the sturgeon, who then go back to eating cats. It could be.

*

People tell me sturgeon stories. A man frying oysters in a restaurant in Portland tells me that his grandpa told him there used to be so many sturgeon in the Columbia that you couldn't use a net because it would for sure get broke whereas the fish were big as cows and there were more of them than a man could count. Hauling in sturgeon, said his grandpa, was like hauling cows to shore, and cows is prettier. A biologist from Texas tells me that sturgeon evolved in their current form long before there was a hint of dinosaur or person in the world. The journalist Richard Carey notes that there are stories of sturgeon in the Volga River in Russia weighing nine thousand pounds, which would be twenty-eight Shaquille O'Neals, and that some sturgeon species can whistle, and that the Kootenai Indians of Idaho used to harpoon sturgeon from canoes they designed to be dragged by the fish until it was exhausted and could be hauled aboard or towed to shore: sturgeon surfing. A Generation Y friend of mine tells me with high glee of the phrases *trout pout* and *sturgeon face*, the former for silicone-injected lippishness and the other for sour visages like those of politicians mournfully explaining how they were on the trail of an Argentinean rather than the Appalachian. One of my many brothers explains Sturgeon's Revelation, named for the science fiction writer Theodore Sturgeon, who said that "ninety percent of everything is crud." A friend of mine who brews beer tells me that the swim bladders of sturgeon are still used by some brewers to clarify beer. An anatomist friend of mine explains that sturgeons have cousins among the bony fishes who emerge from the water and wander around on land for brief periods looking for good things to eat, and that they have other cousins who build up speed to about forty miles an hour underwater and then leap out of the water and glide for more than five hundred feet, which is seventy-one Shaquille O'Neals, and that sturgeons themselves, along with their closest cousins the paddlefish, have such extraordinarily sensitive sensory barbels—the four long whiskerlike tissues between mouth and nose that look not unlike a teenage boy's first uncertain mustache—that they may be able to discern what *kind* of cat they are about to eat. It could be.

*

You would think an essay about a really riveting fish would be by someone who fishes, or would include some actual fishing, or would at least bring you, the esteemed reader, close to the sensory experience of sturgeonness, the shockingly rough sharklike skin so abrasive that those who touch them use work gloves, or how they smell (they even *smell* big, one woman told me), or how their mouths really *do* look and feel like rubber, or how amazingly fast they are when they feel like motoring, or what it feels like to be in a small unstable battered boat in the Columbia River in the pelting winter rain and fish all day and catch nothing except a cold with major hair on it, but I don't fish, for any number of lumbar reasons, and I especially don't want to fish for sturgeon. It's not just that I don't want to be wrenched suddenly toward San Francisco Bay. There's some deeper thing at play that's hard to explain. I don't want to know them that way, you know what I mean? I don't want to hunt them, even for fun. I want to savor them, study them, hear stories, think about them, dig them, grok them, celebrate them. I think I am more interested in sturgeonness than sturgeons. Sometimes you want to see the forest and not the trees. Sometimes you find yourself starving for what's true not about a person but about all people. This is how religion and fascism were born, but it's also why music is the greatest of arts, and why stories matter, and why we all cannot help staring at fires and great waters.

*

I kept coming back to Herman. Every once in a while I would find myself thinking about him and soon I would be in the car sailing through the stunning cliffs and waterfalls of the Columbia Gorge to stand quietly in the shadowy corner of his viewing room for a while. Without fail every time I was there someone would be startled and say something startling. It wasn't always a kid. One time a small man with a Mohawk haircut said something in a language I don't know but his tone was unmistakable and I would bet the house he said *holy shit!* in Mayan or Tagalog. Another time a man knelt and prayed when Herman hove into view. Another time a young woman came in and watched Herman for a while and then gave me a sudden tart lecture on how it was a *sin* and a *crime* to *jail* this fellow living *being* in this ridiculous *circus*, to which I didn't reply, there being nothing to say, and she stomped off.

I went and sat by the river for a long time after that, though. She was right; Herman is in prison for the crime of being amazing, which doesn't seem altogether fair. And for all you can say that he's safe, and well fed, and has lots of visitors to his jail cell, and cool roommates, and a certain renown, especially among children, still, he is confined without cause, and chances are excellent that he would rather be in the river, goofing on salmon and whistling at girl-sturgeon and eating cats and basketballs like the other guys. After a while this bothers me a lot and I get up and shuffle around, my habit when confounded.

I end up at the edge of the Mighty Columbia, which is thought to be maybe ten million years old and which was brawling past this spot, crammed with *Acipenser transmontanus*, long before my forebears wandered out of Africa. A heron lumbers over, looking like a blue tent. In front of me the Bonneville Dam stretches forever. Sturgeon live so long that there are certainly elders above the dam, upriver, who were there before the first lock was built in 1937. Perhaps they are wondering when the sudden wall in the water will dissolve. Perhaps the vast ball of sturgeon that boiled at the base of the dam in early 2008 was not motivated by lust or politics or sea-lion revenge plots but by the itch to communicate with loved ones behind the Wall. No one knows. I go back and watch Herman for a while and I think maybe his job is to be an agent of wonder. Maybe everyone who gapes at Herman gets a sturgeon seed planted in their dreams. Maybe Herman volunteered for the job, or was elected at a confab in the river. Maybe Herman is the one among his clan appointed to awaken the walk-uprights. Maybe he watches the people who watch him and every time a child leaps back amazed Herman scores another one for the good guys. Maybe he is here to grant us humility. Maybe humility and wonder in the right proportions lead to wisdom. It could be.

The Elkometer

Friend of mine out in the woods here in Oregon has invented what he calls the Elkometer, a device to measure, as he says, the proximity, relative health, weight, age, gender, dietary preferences, predation paranoia (by species), and education level of the population of Roosevelt elk living in the vast rain forest abutting his property, which is so deep in the woods your car groans and mutters as you start off on the rutted mud road that leads, after several years, to his slab house, built from fir and cedar he felled himself when we were young.

I asked him what he meant by education level and he pointed out that elk were like any other species, they had a stunning learning curve in their opening scenes on stage, without which, as he said, there would be no Roosevelt elk at all, but sleeker cougars, and who needs that? So the Elkometer measured the pace and volume of epiphany among the young, as he said. How long did it take them to learn to read the winds? When did they learn to watch sentinels when the herd was enduring church service? Were the young males or females quicker to learn the subtle art of picking huckleberries with their lips? The secret to the Elkometer, said my friend, was volume over time; while observation of a few elk was educational, observation of many revealed the beginning of pattern, and pattern is the skeleton of story; so that the Elkometer, at root, was a story machine of startling scope. For example, said my friend, one thing the Elkometer had revealed, after thirty years of use, was that young elk in his valley were more likely to put up a battle when assaulted, as they occasionally were, by bobcats with vaulting ambitions; in his view this tendency among the younger Roosevelts could be traced to twin calves who many years ago pummeled a bobcat, the news spreading mysteriously through the valley. Consider the implications, said my friend. One: elk communicate about assault and battery, who knew? Second: is there a history database among them, or individuals appointed as story keepers, as among human beings? Third: thinner bobcats.

I asked him what other unusual stories the Elkometer has accumulated over the years and he said did you know that elk love Butterfinger bars? I did not know that, he said. I did know that they are idiots for peanut butter, I think for the salt, but I have also discovered over the years that they like tomato juice, beer, and all manner of candy bars, except for, interestingly, Snickers bars, which may be too chewy. They also like jazz but do not like rock music and actively detest country music. Consider the implications: do hunters play country music in their camps, perhaps? Is jazz considered the safest music, evolutionarily? Do elk tend toward Bill Evans at the piano, or Jelly Roll Morton, or, God help us all, Monk?

This is the sort of thing that the Elkometer is designed for, said my friend, as I wrestled with the idea of Roosevelt elk totally digging Thelonious Monk. People think they know a lot about elk, but the Elkometer reveals that we do not hardly know scat. Why are they so much bigger than other elk, for example? A big male Roosevelt can get up to a thousand pounds, which is heroic. Do they have secret food that builds muscle? Are they getting bigger deliberately, maybe to wage war against the cougars? No one knows these things. You can spend a whole life in the woods and never get to know more than a little of the things there are to know. Why are they not afraid of bears at all? Why do they like grapevines so much? Do salal berries, eaten by the ton like elk eat them, lead to jazz? You see the complexity of the problem. Whatever answer you discover to a question just leads to fifty more questions. And that's just with Roosevelt elk. I used to want to ask and answer questions about all sorts of other things, but I realized after a while that all subjects were basically included in Roosevelt elk, which is why I have spent thirty years becoming the Elkometer. Do you have any other questions? Want a Snickers bar?

This Particular Badger

Speaking of badgers, I once spent some time with one, in South Dakota. I was camping with a friend, not far from the *town* of Badger, and I here confess that neither of us was any good at camping, and we had trouble setting up the tent, and making campfires, and the idea of actually *cooking* over the campfire remained a distant dream, which is why we resorted to sandwiches, although one night we did try toasting sandwiches over our feeble flickering campfire, which did not end well, and produced mostly charred shreds of sandwich, which may well be what drew the badger.

He or she joined us during the night; I slowly grew aware of a pronounced chortling and snuffling either in or immediately outside the tent, but the tent was so poorly erected that I could not be sure, and also my tent mate snuffled and grumbled a good deal also, mostly about my poor camping skills, so I was unsure who or what was making the riveting noises either inside or immediately outside the tent. After a while I distinguished the sonorous snoring of my tent mate from the chuffing and muttering outside the tent, and I stepped outside to see who was making all the noise, which sounded very much like the sound an aggrieved uncle poking into the refrigerator after a holiday meal might make if he discovered there were only scraps of turkey and pie left. An aggrieved uncle, in that situation, would make a harrumphing annoyed disgruntled sound, the sound you make when you are poking around in the basement for the saw that was *absolutely* right here not three days ago but which is *certainly* not there now despite *firm* and articulate instructions from the *owner* of the saw that it is *not* to be borrowed for *any* purpose whatsoever without specific *written* permission followed by a three-day *waiting* period while your application is reviewed, and that is exactly the sound I discovered coming from what looked exactly like a large silvery throw-rug nosing around the fire for sandwich shreds.

I realized quickly, even in the dim light, that this was almost certainly not a throw-rug that had come to life, and that it was probably a badger, although you never saw a badger that looked more like a large disheveled rug in your whole life. If you had a rug that used to be thick and white, but which had suffered the slings and arrows of fate over the years, and had never been properly washed, and had begun to fray and tatter at the edges, and had been rushed headlong through the wilderness so that it had accumulated twigs and bits of leaves and even some pebbles and old teeth, and sap or jelly or blood had coagulated in a couple of places and created snarls that would have mystified Houdini, and then the rug had been given hundreds of dust baths, and been used by a clumsy matador, and then been set upon by a Lutheran with an attitude, then you would have a rug that looked exactly like this particular badger, although this badger had a small pointed head, which few rugs have.

I said something insipid to the badger, probably about sports, as I recall, and he or she glared up at me and then hurried off into the darkness, looking unbelievably like your bedroom rug deciding suddenly to go downstairs and see if there's any pie left from dinner. So that was the end of the time I spent with a badger. Since then I have spent no time with badgers, not from lack of interest but more from lack of opportunity, and if ever I get the chance to meet a badger again, you can be sure I will not open the conversation with sports. The fact is, no matter what you think, or what odd sound you make deep in your throat like you swallowed a squirrel and now are thinking better of it, that not everyone is interested in sports.

Cyrus

Recently I was in Arkansas, near the Oklahoma border, and a shy man told me a story that I cannot forget; so I share it with you this morning.

I had the best mule that ever was, said the shy man. That mule was a wonder. I called him Cyrus although I believe that was not his true name. I believe his true name was probably the sound the other mules made respectfully when they came upon him in the fields or on the road. You could tell the sound they made was some sort of respectful title for Cyrus, like sir or governor. He was something like the chieftain of the mules for miles around my farm. I used to farm four hundred acres, most of which was woods, and the farms around me were mostly woods also, so a lot of the time Cyrus and me were in the woods, and even the little animals in the woods were respectful of Cyrus. Raccoons and deer and such would skitter out of the way when we came through, same as they usually do, but then they would stand alongside the road and nod to Cyrus. You think maybe I am telling you a fiction but I am not. My bride noticed this too on her own the times she took Cyrus out to haul logs and such. The only animals that were not respectful of Cyrus were the bigger animals like cougars and bears, and there was an elk lived over to Oklahoma that one time tried to attack Cyrus but that did not come off, as Cyrus stood his ground.

That mule was a wonder. No one knew how he came to be what he was but he just was. He was a fine worker and not as testy as your usual mule. Your usual mule is generally displeased because of his complex family history—not as thoroughly displeased as a donkey, of course, but generally unhappy with his lot—but this was not so with Cyrus. My bride came to love him deeply for what she called his inarguable character. She says that there is personality and then there is character, and the one is a pond and the other is a sea. She says even *chickens* can have personalities, whereas character is a reverence. She too noticed the respect in which Cyrus was held by all sorts of other beings. I remarked once that he was something like the emperor of all the mules for miles around but she said it was more than that, that all sorts of people also had the greatest respect for Cyrus, and that perhaps he was a sage or a saint in ways we sensed but did not understand. She says we don't know much at all about how this works. She says we talk about *humans* being sages and saints but we don't think at all about sages and saints among the other beings, and who is to say that there are not sages and saints covered with fur and feathers? I say do you mean fishes too, and she says good heavens no! and we laugh. But I think she was right about Cyrus.

Well, he got old and died, sure he did. Mules get old and die like anybody else. Cyrus took a long time to get old, though. He was forty when he retired and fifty when he died. This was a Tuesday. He had free rein of the farm, of course, and he came out of the woods and over to the house and called to us to come out and then he lay down in the grass. We all gathered around and after a while he died. We buried him in the woods, among the pin oaks. He sure liked pin oaks. He liked all sorts of oaks, bur oak and red oak and white oak, but he liked pin oaks the best, so that's where he is. I go out there almost every day still and you would be surprised how many tracks of animals you see there, all sorts of animals, little and big, even the bears and cougars. I never have seen elk tracks there though. I don't know what it was between Cyrus and the elks, and now I guess I will never know.

Joyas Volardores

Consider the hummingbird for a long moment. A hummingbird's heart beats ten times a second. A hummingbird's heart is the size of a pencil point. A hummingbird's heart is most of the hummingbird. *Joyas volardores,* flying jewels, the first white explorers in the Americas called them, and the white men had never seen such creatures, for hummingbirds came into the world only in the Americas, only here, nowhere else in the universe, more than three hundred species of them whirring and zooming and nectaring in hummer time zones nine times removed from ours, their hearts hammering faster than we could clearly hear were our elephantine ears pressed to their infinitesimal chests.

*

Each one visits a thousand flowers a day. They can dive at sixty miles an hour. They can fly backwards. They can fly more than five hundred miles without pausing to rest. But when they rest they come close to death: on frigid nights, or when they are starving, they retreat into torpor, their metabolic rate slowing to a fifteenth of their normal sleep rate, their hearts sludging nearly to a halt, barely beating, and if they are not soon warmed, if they do not soon find that which is sweet, their hearts grow cold, and they cease to be. Consider for a moment those hummingbirds who did not open their eyes again today, this very day, in the Americas: bearded helmetcrests and booted racket-tails, violet-tailed sylphs and violet-capped woodnymphs, crimson topazes and purple-crowned fairies, red-tailed comets and amethyst woodstars, rainbow-bearded thornbills and glittering-bellied emeralds, velvet-purple coronets and golden-bellied star-frontlets, fiery-tailed awlbills and Andean hillstars, spatuletails and pufflegs, each the most amazing thing you have never seen, each thunderous wild heart the size of the tiniest pebble, each mad heart silent, a brilliant music stilled.

*

Hummingbirds, like all flying birds but more so, have incredible enormous immense ferocious metabolisms. To drive those metabolisms they have race-car hearts that eat oxygen at an eye-popping rate. Their hearts are built of thinner leaner fibers than ours. Their arteries are stiffer and more taut. They have more mitochondria in their heart muscles. Anything to gulp more oxygen. Their hearts are stripped to the skin for the war against gravity and inertia, the mad search for food, the insane idea of flight. The price of their ambition is a life closer to death; they suffer heart attacks and aneurysms and ruptures more than any other living creature. It's expensive to fly. You burn out. You fry the machine. You melt the engine. Every creature on earth has approximately two billion heartbeats to spend in a lifetime. You can spend them slowly, like a tortoise, and live to be two hundred years old, or you can spend them fast, like a hummingbird, and live to be two years old.

*

The biggest heart in the world is inside the blue whale. It weighs more than seven tons. It's as big as a room. It *is* a room, with four chambers. A child could walk around in it, head high, bending only to step through the valves. The valves are as big as the swinging doors in a saloon. This house of a heart drives a creature a hundred feet long. When this creature is born, it is twenty feet long and weighs four tons. It is *way* bigger than your car. It drinks a hundred gallons of milk from its mama every day and gains two hundred pounds a day and when it is seven or eight years old, it endures an unimaginable puberty and then it essentially disappears from human ken, for next to nothing is known of the mating habits, travel patterns, diet, social life, language, social structure, diseases, spirituality, wars, stories, despairs, and arts of the blue whale. There are perhaps ten thousand blue whales in the world, living in every ocean on earth, and of the largest mammal who ever lived we know nearly nothing. But we know this: the animals with the largest hearts in the world generally travel in pairs, and their penetrating moaning cries, their piercing yearning tongue, can be heard underwater for miles and miles.

*

Mammals and birds have hearts with four chambers. Reptiles and turtles have hearts with three chambers. Fish have hearts with two chambers. Insects and mollusks have hearts with one chamber. Worms have hearts with one chamber, although they may have as many as eleven one-chambered hearts. Unicellular bacteria have no hearts at all; but even they have fluid eternally in motion, washing from one side of the cell to the other, swirling and whirling. No living being is without interior liquid motion. We all churn inside.

*

So much held in a heart in a life. So much held in a heart in a day, an hour, a moment. We are utterly open with no one, in the end—not mother and father, not wife or husband, not lover, not child, not friend. We open windows to each but we live alone in the house of the heart. Perhaps we must. Perhaps we could not bear to be so naked, for fear of a constantly harrowed heart. When young we think there will come one person who will savor and sustain us always; when we are older we know this is the dream of a child, that all hearts finally are bruised and scarred, scored and torn, repaired by time and will, patched by force of character, yet fragile and rickety forevermore, no matter how ferocious the defense and how many bricks you bring to the wall. You can brick up your heart as stout and tight and hard and cold and impregnable as you possibly can and down it comes in an instant, felled by a woman's second glance, a child's apple breath, the shatter of glass in the road, the words *I have something to tell you*, a cat with a broken spine dragging itself into the forest to die, the brush of your mother's papery ancient hand in the thicket of your hair, the memory of your father's voice early in the morning echoing from the kitchen where he is making pancakes for his children.

Raptorous

I have been so hawk-addled and owl-absorbed and falcon-haunted and eagle-maniacal since I was a little kid that it was a huge shock to me to discover that there are people who couldn't care less about the clan of raptor—those arrows and bolts of razor-fingered fury in the sky, those masters of the air, those gleaners of meat in bushes and fields. I couldn't get over it. There were kids who did not think that seeing a sparrowhawk helicoptering over an empty lot and then dropping like a tiny anvil and o my god *coming up with wriggling lunch* wasn't the coolest thing ever?

I mean, who could possibly not be awed by a tribe whose various members could see a rabbit clearly from a mile away (eagles), who could fly sideways though tree branches like feathered fighter planes (the wood hawks), who looked like tiny brightly colored linebackers (kestrels, with their cool gray helmets), who hunted absolutely silently on the wing (owls), who flew faster than any other being on earth (falcons), and who could spot a whopping trout from fifty feet in the air, gauge piscine speed and direction, and nail the dive and light-refraction and wind-gust and trout-startle so perfectly that it snags three fish a day (our friend the osprey)? Not to mention they *looked* cool—they were seriously large, they had muscles on their muscles, they were stone-cold efficient hunters with built-in butchery tools, they weren't afraid of anything or anyone, and all of them had this stern *I could kick your ass but I am busy* look, which took me years to discover was not a general simmer of testiness but a result of the supraorbital ridge protecting their eyes.

To me as a child and ever after they were more *adamant* than other birds—lovely and amazing as their many cousins were, from the gawky glory of herons to the speed-freak entertainment of wrens and bushtits. They arrested your attention. You saw a hawk, you stopped what you were doing and paid attention to a master of its craft, who commanded the horizon until he or she was done with the moment and drifted airily away. You saw an eagle, you gaped; you heard the piecing whistle of an osprey along the river, you stood still and listened with reverence; you saw an owl launch at dusk, like a burly gray dream against the russet last light, you flinched a little, and were awed, and counted yourself blessed.

They inspire fear, too—that should be said. They are hunters, they carry switchblades and know how to use them, they back down from no one, and there are endless stories of eagles carrying away babies left unattended for a fateful moment in meadows and clearings, and falcons shearing off the eyebrows of idiots climbing to their nests, and hawks and owls swooping in to snatch appetizer-size kittens, and owls casually biting off the fingers of people who discover Fluffy is actually Ferocious. A friend of mine deep in the Oregon forest, for example, tells the story of watching a gyrfalcon descend upon his chickens, and grab a fat one with a daggered fist as big as my friend's fist but with better weaponry, and rise again easily into the fraught and holy air, while glaring at my friend with the clear message, as my friend says, with something like reverence, *I am taking this chicken, and you are not going to be a fool and mess with me.* You wouldn't believe how clear and articulate the message was, says my friend, who still tells this story with awe in his voice, and he is a burly guy who has messed with bears and cougars and lived to tell stories about that.

I suppose what I am talking about here really is awe and reverence and some kind of deep thrumming respect for beings who are very good at what they do and fit into this world with admirable sinewy grace. We are all hunters, in the end, bruised and battered and broken in various ways, and we seek always to rise again, and fit deftly into the world, and soar to our uppermost reaches, enduring with as much grace as we can. Maybe the reason that so many human beings are as hawk-addled and owl-absorbed and falcon-haunted and eagle-maniacal as me is because in a real way we wish to live like them, to use them like stars to steer by, to remember to be as alert and unafraid as they are. Maybe being raptorous is in some way rapturous. Maybe what the word *rapture* really means is an attention so ferocious that you see the miracle of the world as the miracle it is. Maybe that is what happens to saints and mystics who float up into the air and soar beyond sight and vanish finally into the glare of the sun.

Reading the Birds

Big birds: A golden eagle, huge and huddled, its head drawn down between its shoulders against hissing snow, standing forlornly on a pine branch like a sorrowful monk. Two young bald eagles, not yet hooded with white, launching together from a Sitka spruce like two immense prayers; the bough they gripped shivers for a moment, remembering. A red-tailed hawk the size of a toddler sliding from an oak snag onto a rabbit; the rabbit screams twice, a thin awful whistle; the hawk drapes its wings over the scene like a curtain. Last, largest, a baleful condor in a zoo cage, staring at awed children, its unblinking hooded yellow eyes forgetting nothing.

Small birds: A hummingbird the color of joy. A wren in a winter thicket, a circle amid lines. A sparrow, tiny and cocky, shouting at cars and dogs. A finch pouring summer from its mouth. A tree swallow, no bigger than the hand of a child, carving the huge air into circles of iridescent green and blue and black. It swims and slices through the air. It is as light as a whip tip. It is made of sunlight and insect juice, exuberance, and desire.

*

Once, years ago, I had my own woods. My wife and I were caretakers of the house that anchored them, that rose above them like a shambling wooden castle. The house and its woods stood on a muscle of earth called Snake Hill.

I spent a great deal of time in the woods of Snake Hill, collecting kindling, tracking pheasants in snow, reading the runes of twigs. Many twilights I stood and watched buttery last light spatter through oaks, birches, beeches. One evening I noticed five immense birds in a maple. They were huddled together like a feathered fist. They were nearly three feet tall, they hunched their heads like shy children, they lurched out of the tree at dusk with the gracelessness of small sofas. But they were not graceless long; within a second or two they unfurled their enormous wings and flapped away croaking, groaning, sobbing. Far below I gaped at their huge silhouettes against the corduroy sky.

They were night herons. I learned this from a neighbor who knew his neighbors. We stood under the tree one night and watched the herons soar away. It was my neighbor's firm opinion that we should know the names of our neighbors, that residence entailed self-education, that full life in a place meant knowing the creatures of that place. He believed that stories were ways to live, and so he collected and told stories with an eagerness that belied his age and failing health.

Those five feathered stories meant a great deal to me. Sitting in my trees, slicing through the woolen twilight, they blessed my house, my land, my residence on Snake Hill. They added awe and savor to the woods. They excited the landscape, underlined its wildness, underscored the fact that it belonged to no one and was only borrowed by the house and people in its midst.

*

Wimbledon, England, some years ago. Eventual Lawn Tennis Champion Stefan Edberg of Sweden winds up for a backhand return to his opponent, Boris Becker of Germany. Suddenly a pied wagtail, a tiny British bird, zooms right across Edberg's line of vision, perhaps a foot from his face. He hits his shot deep into the stands, then scowls, then laughs. The television announcer informs the audience worldwide that a family of pied wagtails has taken up residence in Centre Court's eaves. The British, ever respectful of hearth and home, have not seen fit to evict the birds.

Starlings take up residence in eaves, dryers, garages, attics, air conditioner vents. The tiny flycatchers called phoebes set up nests on porch lights. So do barn swallows. Swallows and barn owls live in barns, tool sheds, abandoned farmhouses, unattended shacks. Guillemots live on abandoned docks and wharves and wrecks. Peregrine falcons nest on skyscrapers and bridges. Pigeons live under bridges and highway abutments. I remember the house sparrows that lived for years in our garage when I was a boy; their eggs fell from the roof every spring like slow blue rain.

Once, on a wet Easter morning, I found a fallen sparrow chick on the concrete floor of the garage. It was a male, about a week old. He was twisted, small, deceased. Sometime during the night he had fallen, or been shoved by his siblings, from their disheveled nest in the eaves. My brothers and I buried him in a crayon box. We prayed over the gaudy coffin. My youngest brother sobbed uncontrollably. The broken chick did not rise from the dead, as we hoped but did not expect. Ever after, says my brother, he looked upon Jesus with a jaundiced eye, and wondered at the potency of a story that could not stir life in something so small as a shriveled sparrow.

*

Human beings are attached to the world by intricate strings of memory and desire. We make of our sensory impressions the stuff of a life, a career, a love affair, a story. Birds are players in this drama; they flit about us, encapsulating the ways that we feel, acting as poems, as prayers. I once cried at the sight of a sparrow's defiant, thin-legged stance because it was a speck of unbearable delight in a black time.

Perhaps birds are most powerful poems for the youngest human beings. The writer Richard Lewis, director of a children's art center in New York City, annually has his young students make bird masks and don them and then tell stories about the birds that they are. "My bird is in you," said Joel, eight years old. "His name is imagination. He lives in a place called heart brain body. It is in everyone. Some adults think it is childish but it will never leave you even if you hide it."

Birds are in us, in our stories of ourselves. Raven stole the sun from heaven and gave it to the Northwest Indian tribes. Eagle gave the Iroquois the dew, made the wind for the Chippewa, tore Prometheus's liver from his body day after day. Wrens and cranes fly through the legends of Saint Kevin of Glendalough, swallows and doves through stories of Saint Francis, crows through the lore of the Desert Fathers.

They are still in our stories. The day after my father-in-law died, his widow noticed a robin persistently trying to enter their house through what had been her husband's favorite window. The bird tried to get in for a week, always through the same window. I explained to her that the robin, an aggressively territorial bird in season, was probably trying to drive off the intruder he saw reflected in the glass. She listened politely and was not convinced. Ever after there is a soft place in her heart for robins. For her they are symbols, messages, memories in feathered jackets; for her robins are bits of her husband, whom she loved desperately and completely, whom she misses most in spring, when robins return and he does not.

*

I have seen many eagles, none low or reduced to this dimension, each lord of the immediate air. They freeze the creatures below them. I have seen a yearling blacktail deer flinch when an eagle's cold shadow passed by. Recently I stood on a high hill in Sitka spruce country, on the Oregon coast, trying to read history by trees: ancient hemlocks in inaccessible ravines, second-growth spruce near trails, alder and brush on open hillsides. Suddenly, silently, two bald eagles were above me. Their shadows swept over the woods, over thickets of salal, salmonberry, blackberry. The hills held their breath. One eagle screamed twice; both eagles slid over the ridgeline and were gone; a wren piped; time resumed.

Walt Whitman saw bald eagles once, over his native Long Island. They were performing their mating dance, a violent swirling waltz conducted wholly in air. Old Walt, characteristically, got the sight down in one enormous sentence. "Skyward in air a sudden muffled sound, the dalliance of the eagles," he wrote. "The rushing amorous contact high in space together, the clinching interlocking claws, a living, fierce, gyrating wheel, four beating wings, two beaks, a swirling mass tight grappling, in tumbling turning clustering loops, straight downward falling, till o'er the river pois'd, the twain yet one, a moment's lull, a motionless still balance in the air, then parting, talons loosing, upward again on slow-firm pinions slanting, their separate diverse flight, she hers, he his, pursuing."

She hers, he his, pursuing.

*

They are creatures from other universes, performing physical feats we can only imagine. A peregrine falcon in full stoop upon a duck is the fastest autonomous creature in the history of the world, reaching speeds of perhaps two hundred miles an hour just before it collides with its prey. It has been designed, over many thousands of years, to be a bullet of feathers and toothpick bones and knife-fingers. A golden eagle can see a rabbit's ear twitch from two miles away. A screech owl can hear a mouse running one hundred feet away. An albatross, nine feet wing-wide, spends nearly its entire life floating over the ocean; it sleeps on the wing, dozing amid billows. The rufous-sided hummingbird, the common tiny hummer of the Pacific

Northwest, has a heartbeat rate of some three hundred beats per minute—about five times as fast as the human heartbeat. (*"Everything* about a hummingbird is a superlative," wrote the naturalist Tom Colazo.)

The implications of its heartbeat intrigue me. Does the hummingbird live faster than we do? Does the hummingbird literally live in a different time zone? Time must be made of a different liquid for the hummingbird, since he goes through it so quickly. I imagine my life running five times faster. It seems to run too fast now, and I am a man with a peaceable wife and one small child.

*

The first word my daughter learned, other than the labels she has used since for her parents, was *Bird*. I think this is because birds moved across her nascent vision in delightful ways. I spent many hours, in her first few months, holding her against my shoulder so that she could see out a large window. The window overlooks cedar, fir, spruce, laurel, honeysuckle. In the trees and bushes live sparrows, juncoes, warblers, jays, starlings, flickers, robins, crows. The trees are green, the bushes are red, the birds are Joseph's coat. In the chimney of the house next door are brick-brown chimney swifts, which issue forth in a dark cloud at dusk. They swirl and swim in the air like dreams.

Many times I shifted a bit in my chair and felt my daughter's pumpkin head resting against my shoulder and assumed she had fallen asleep, and then turned slightly to see her eyes, and saw them wide open and filled with birds. One day she told me what she saw, muttering wetly in my ear, her feathery voice a pale blue sound, a faint fluted note from a new country. Bird, she whispered, Bird Bird.

Now, a year later, when she sees Bird she does not name

him, but blows him a kiss, as she does to family and friends. She holds her fingers over her tiny pursed lips and then swings her hand out and away into the air. Her linked fingers float in the air for a curved instant like a wing.

*

They are travelers beyond our imagination. I once lived along the New England shore, in the middle of what ornithologists call the Atlantic Flyway. Every September hundreds of thousands of birds funneled through the air over my head. Hawks, eagles, falcons, and vultures, while only a fraction of the millions of birds sailing along the coast, are the biggest and most dramatic of the migrants. Ordinarily solitary hunters, they band together in the fall not from camaraderie but because they all ride rising columns of warm air along ridges and hills. From September through November it's possible to see hundreds, sometimes thousands, of hawks and falcons rising together from the woods, a reverse rain of raptors, all intent on gaining soaring height for their trips to Central and South America.

For the raptors this little autumnal jaunt can mean two thousand miles in the air. The arctic tern sneers at that trip; it travels from one pole to the other in its migration. Other birds travel short distances thoroughly. Hummingbirds have rectangular territories a few yards wide. Wrens have slightly larger territories, perhaps a hundred yards square. Western jays have territories with ceilings: at sea level is the scrub jay, in the woods is the Steller's jay, at high elevations is the whiskeyjack, or camp robber, and at the tree line is Clark's nutcracker, the jay closest to heaven. (The bird is named for Captain William Clark, the first white man to describe it, and the first white man to stand on the bluff where a university is situated today; Clark himself was led to the Northwest by a Shoshoni woman named

Sacagawea, or Bird Woman.) In a single vertical mile there may
be four jay territories, each inviolate, bound only by elevation
above the sea. To travel well within your neighborhood, said
Samuel Johnson, is the greatest of journeys.

*

I work at a university perched on a high bluff over the Wil-
lamette River. Across the river is a line of velvet hills punctuated
by soaring hawks; below the campus is the sinuous gleam of the
river, a highway for creaking flotillas of great blue herons. The
campus itself is a village of many species: students, professors,
employees, cars, insects, trees, birds. Students and birds are the
most exuberant. The students chirp, preen, molt, congregate
in gaggles and flocks, perform bizarre courtship dances. The
birds study insects, analyze traffic patterns, edit lawns, flutter
through classrooms. Some birds live in residence halls; others
commute to the university. I have seen nests in eaves, nests in
pipes, nests in windows.

The space in which I type these words was an empty attic
corner two years ago. Where my fingers rise and fall there was
a pigeon nest. Perhaps there has been life in this corner of the
building since 1891, when it was built. One year it stood empty
and there were goats in the halls. Then this floor was a dormi-
tory filled with boys. Then it was a biology laboratory filled
with animals and insects. Then it was a place where the wind
lived. Now I live here on weekdays, and under the window
where there were pigeons there is me, writing about birds, my
fingers fluttering.

*

In the ancient days of falconry, according to the Abbess Ju-
liana Berners, there was a hierarchy of bird possession: eagles
were for emperors, gyrfalcons for kings, peregrine falcons
for earls, merlins for ladies, goshawks for yeomen, kestrels

(sparrow hawks) for priests, and muskets (woodland hawks) for altar servers. Those days of yore were the halycon days of falconry, the art by which raptors are trained to the hand. Probably this ancient art began as a means to procure food, but by the Abbess's day falconry was a pastime fully as ritualistic and as filled with lore as any religion, and the reaping of rabbits and birds for the pot was incidental to the training and flying of the hawks themselves. No craft of the medieval ages was as respected, and none led to as many arguments about the best way to practice the art. It was King James I, the fellow for whom the King James Bible is named, who noted that falconry is an extreme stirrer-up of passions. "That is because the hawks themselves are furious creatures, and the people who associate with them catch it," wrote T. H. White, whose book *The Goshawk* is both meditation on the poetry of raptors and modern manual for their training to the fist.

Of all birds I love the raptors best. They are the most dramatic, the largest, among the most intelligent. Falconers say that raptors are fully capable of love, hate, and violent emotional instability. They are creatures that veer wildly from love to hate, that eat their fellow creatures, that soar in the sky and squabble in the mud, that care tenderly for their infants and battle with their adolescents, that reportedly can love, lust, laugh, play, mourn, wage war, speak a language, and endure depression.

I think that they are my cousins.

*

We eat birds. We have eaten them for many thousands of years. Chickens, pheasants, game hens, sparrows, pigeons, doves, quail, chukar, turkeys, hens, geese, grouse, ducks, larks. We have eaten nearly every bird that flies or swims or runs; it may be that we have eaten at least one of every species of bird.

(Occasionally one *person* tries to eat every species of bird: King Richard's menu for a weekend jaunt to his country home, in the year 1387, included 5 herons, 50 swans, 96 capons, 110 geese, 192 pullets, 240 cranes and curlews, 720 hens, and 1,200 peacocks.) Birds die for us by the billions. They become feasts, cures, salvifics, sandwiches, soup. Their bodies stave off our hunger and sadness. The writer M. F. K. Fisher tells the tale of the Maréchal de Mouchy, who returned home from the funeral of his best friend and ordered two roast pigeons for dinner. "I have noticed that after eating a brace of pigeons I arise from the table feeling much more resigned," he said to his cook. His cook, if frugal, probably took the remnants of the roast birds and made soup, perhaps to succor a sick child, perhaps to savor on a cold winter afternoon, when all seems bleak and dead, and steaming soup may lift the heart.

*

They *fly*. They go where we cannot go. They lift themselves into the air and dream away. A simple process: Weighing next to nothing, hollow-boned, with lung capacities a hundred times greater than ours, they swim into the air and stay there, their wings marshalling what poet William Blake called the First Element. Their wings are curiously human in bone structure: The outstretched arm of an albatross could be that of a basketball player—radius, ulna, humerus, carpus, hand, fingers. My friend Marlene, who teaches biology, tells me she always used birds as examples when teaching bone structure. No other creature, she says, made such an immediate impact on students. Once in a while she would notice a student surreptitiously extend his arm like a wing, seeing his own appendage with new eyes, flexing his fingers up like a hawk surfing a thermal.

*

They are what we once were: vigorous creatures fully immersed in the physical world. For better, I think, human beings long ago grew out of that immersion, and strove toward a different world, one of reason, one of the spirit. But we do well when we pay attention to our forebears, who are exuberant; we do evil when we cast them aside as appendages, servants, underlings, tools. We are ourselves underlings to something vast, and a scrabbling for power among servants is a battle of children in dust.

In them is poetry, energy, exuberance; in them is life, pure and untrammeled, unadulterated and holy. We learn most and best about life by contemplating life; that is why we stare achingly at our children as they sleep, that is why our happiest moments are those spent in the arms and hearts of those who love us, that is why we are inexplicably pleased when a sparrow pauses for a second at the window and regards us with an irrepressible eye. Small as she is, she is our teacher and our companion, our fellow tatter torn from the cloak of the Maker. She is a small vigorous prayer, a hymn with wings, a laugh given life and set aloft.

II.

Brief Inquiries & Observances of the
Wilder Animals We Call Children for Lack of a
Better Generic Label for Those Most Headlong
of Mammals; with Sidelong Glances at
Human Beings & the Seething Roaring
Natural World in Which We Swim

＊

The Slather

Here, I'll *prove* to you that there are no tiny moments, no dull moments, no little things, only a general failure on our parts to see the wild and amazing slather of miracles that come unbidden and will, for each of us, too soon end, all too soon; But not yet.

Yesterday I was idling in the social ramble, in a rare splurge of sunshine here in the Pacific North Wet—a burst of light so startling that people emerged dewy from their mossy holes and mooed in delight and held crucifixes and talismans aloft in praise and fear—and I noticed a child, age one and change, crawling free in the ocean of the grass; she was remotely attended by her father, who kept one eye on the scuttle of his daughter, rotating that eye exactly like a lizard does; but otherwise she ranged loose in the swell of the lawn, and I grew interested in her voyage and watched as her skin grew greener and her jumper soaked with dew; but there was one moment when the heavens opened not from above, as usual, but from the chambers of my heart, the doors of which are sometimes rusted shut for any number of reasons, all of them reasonable and all of them foolish, in the end; and of that moment I alone am here to tell thee.

She paused in her jaunt and journey, this small ship of a child, and scrabbled in the moist, and hauled forth a caterpillar with a coat of many colors, and hoisted it into view—her eyes still so fresh from the amazement factory that you could almost see the warranty tag—and she exclaimed with delight, and then she ate the caterpillar ever so gently, placing it in the holy cave of her mouth with reverence, and closing her tiny lips with honest pleasure, and savoring the interior wriggle of her guest; and then she pursed the tiny bud of her lips as if for a kiss, and the caterpillar was extruded, or ejected, or escaped, or was essentially whistled back into the ocean of the grass, into which he or she vanished with an alacrity I had never noticed in caterpillars before, which may be characteristic of that species, or which may have been a reaction of this one caterpillar to what we must call unimaginable circumstances, it being unlikely that caterpillars are versed in the legend of Jonah and the whale, despite the story appearing not only in the Bible but in the Qur'an, long may it wave.

A small girl, a caterpillar, a young crew cut father who soon thereafter scooped up his progeny, and cradled her in the crook and burl of his arm, and that was inarguably that, and the day trundled on apace. But there was a child, whom no science can fully explain, for there never was a being like her in billions of years before she arrived, nor will there be such a being again, no matter how long the worlds do spin in the measureless void; and there was a caterpillar, so brilliantly hued and crammed with incipient flight that we can only gape and wonder that such a creature liveth in the profligate world we share; and there was a sea of gleaming grass so rife with life that a herd of mathematicians would age and wither before that sum was calculated; and there was a young dad, with a sensory apparatus so remarkable that he knew exactly how many inches his daughter was from his harbor, and exactly the instant she should be retrieved and dried and given to suck; and there was a slight grizzled man with a glass of excellent wine, watching the gift of all this, a man so amazed and astounded and moved that he had to put down his goblet and retire to the men's room to brim with joy that such things are in this world, and are given to us to see and savor; so it is that we are blessed beyond measure, which you know and I know; but we cannot, I think, be reminded enough.

Tigers

I am standing in the hospital watching babies emerge from my wife like a circus act. First one out is a boy, dark-haired and calm, the size of an owl. He is immediately commandeered by a nurse who whisks him off for a bath and a stint in what appears to be a tiny tanning bed.

Now, says the doctor, reaching around inside my wife while he talks, here's the other one, and he hauls out another boy. This one is light-haired and not calm; he grabs for a nurse's scissors and won't let go and they have to pry his fingers off and the nurse looks accusingly at me for some reason and I want to say *hey, I don't even know the guy,* but I don't say anything, being overwhelmed with new roommates and tears and astonishment at people emerging from my wife one after another like a circus act.

This boy, the second one, the burglar, turns out to have a major heart problem. He's missing a chamber in his heart. You need four chambers, and most people get four, but he only gets three, and there's no one to whom I can complain, so they have to fix him, otherwise he dies.

Fixing him entails cutting open his chest with a saw and prying the chest bone open with a tool that looks like the Jaws of Life and chilling his heart with a bucket of ice and hooking him up to a machine that continues to pump his blood and some of mine through his brain and body while the surgeon reroutes his veins.

I ask if I can hold him in my lap during the operation, just to have my skin on his skin while he goes off to another planet while they fix him, but they say no.

Outside the hospital window I see three crows dogging a hawk. The hawk flinches when they flare by his head, he ducks and rolls and hunches his shoulders, but he doesn't leave the tree. His troubles are inches from his face but he glares and waits, stolid, angry, churning, his thoughts sharp as razors, his brain filled with blood and meat.

The operation is really two operations, it turns out, and the doctors do the first one pretty soon after he's born, and that operation goes by in a blur, and then there's a second operation, when he's almost two years old, and that goes by in a blur too, although I remember finding a nurse praying by his crib at four in the morning when I go to pray by his crib.

A day after the second operation the doctors tell me I can try to feed him real food, the food he likes, which is peas.

So here I am feeding him in his hospital bed. The bed is cantilevered up at the north end so that he can eat. He is eating pea by pea. He is awake but groggy and each time a pea hoves into his viewfinder he regards it with sluggish surprise. He likes peas. I put the peas in his mouth one by one. His lips reach out a little for each pea and then maul it gently for a while before the pea disappears. Each time his lips accept the pea they also accept the ends of my thumb and forefinger for an instant. After thirteen peas he falls asleep and I crank the bed back flat and kneel down and pray like hell.

Next day the doctors say I can heft him gently out of his bed and hold him, just be careful with all the wires and tubes. There are a lot of wires and tubes. There is a heart monitor with wires running from his chest to a machine the size of a dryer. There is a breathing tube planted in his nose. There is a blood pressure monitor attached to his big toe. There is a drainage tube running from his chest to a clear plastic box on the end of his bed. The box fills twice a day with blood and water. There is a tube in his neck, in his carotid artery. This tube runs nowhere. It's for emergencies. It's the tube through which the doctor would cram major drugs in case the surgical repair of his heart fails, slumps over, gives out, blows a tire, pops a gasket, gives up the ghost, kicks the bucket, hits the wall, buys the farm.

I lift him out of the bed. He whimpers and moans. I feel like my fingers are knives on him, but I fold him into my lap and we settle back into the recliner and arrange the wires and tubes so that no machines are beeping. I grab the clicker and flip on the television, which hangs from the ceiling like a goiter. *Click* bass fishing *click* talk show *click* infomercial *click* news *click* nature show *click* basketball game *click* sit-com *click* commercial at which point the boy who has been slumped in my lap like a dozing seal suddenly reaches for the clicker, startling me; I thought he was asleep. But no—he punches away at the clicker with his thumb and back down the channels we go, *click* sit-com *click* basketball game *click* nature show, which is about tigers, and having arrived at the tigers he wanted to see, he stops clicking, leans back into my lap again,

and laughs!

a guttural chortle, a deep-in-the-throat guffaw, a basso *huh huh huh*, and a great sob rises in me suddenly, and for the next few minutes, as we watch the massive grace and power and patience of tigers, I cry like the baby he used to be before all these tubes and wires, because this is the first time he's laughed in weeks, and he is going to be fine, and everything is suddenly over.

A few minutes later when he grows tired of tigers and the excitement of being out of bed he moans again and I put him back in the bed and arrange his nest of wires and tubes, and he is already asleep by the time I flip out the light and stand against the window and lean forward and touch the window with my face and think about hawks and tigers and pray like crazy.

The Hymn of Him

Begin with my infant son peeing in my right eye. Yes—let's start there. It's an unforgettable image, isn't it? And it actually happened. Who cares what year and what city and what time of day? He was six months old and fatter than the later Marlon Brando and I peeled his moist stuff off and leaned over him to blow raspberries into his capacious belly to make him snicker and up periscope! and fire at will, captain! Good thing I wear spectacles, is all I can say.

As I remember he then guffawed and after a minute of recovery so did I, and later when I was soaking my spectacles for a really long time in boiling water his wry and gentle mother asked me what I was doing and when I explained she laughed so hard she had to go lie down for a while. This actually happened also.

The thing is, though, that I am not just *reporting* this, or trying to recreate the moment, or telling you this story to escort us both toward a cool theme or conclusion near the end of the page. Nope: I want the *moment* again, fresh and wild and hilarious. I want it so bad I can taste the stony chalky desperate of it. I don't want to remember it; *I want it again right now before this sentence ends.* If I write it I'll have it again.

Here, stand with me at the changing table by the window. Here's my son, thirty inches tall and naked as a worm after rain. Lean down with me, toward his belly like a pale beach, like the skull of a seal, and we'll babble right into it, and he will chortle that deep laugh like a bear with a head cold, and then o *sweet jesus!*

Or here he is being issued a citation by a cop. Or here he is on a surgeon's table. Or here he is on the couch under the blanket with his girlfriend and they are not watching the basketball game like they said they were, and when I come in to deliver clean folded towels and check the score (it's a crucial playoff game), I do *not* deliver the towels and do *not* check the score. *Here he is,* is what I am trying to say, right here in these sentences. As long as I write a sentence with him in it he is in it. In this sentence he is a reckless fool. In this next one he is a sweet wild holy brilliant gentle witty delight. In this third sentence we are sitting at the old ash table in the cracked golden light after dinner and he is lying to me about his test paper and I know he is lying and he knows I know and I am so angry that I get up and leave this sentence. Here we are in the backyard listening to osprey whistling overhead and he is a miracle in my lap. Here he is tall and thin and folding his mother into his long lean chest as she sobs after her mother died. Here he is being man enough to say calmly he messed up and it's his fault and there's no one else to blame. Here is a sentence in which he is so drunk that his grim twin brother has to carry him in his arms to bed. *Here he is* in every sentence and as long as I keep writing sentences every one is the hymn of him.

Some sentences are starving for the things inside the sentences. Some sentences are love slathered in ink. Some sentences try to give birth to things we cannot say. Some sentences reach for things they cannot ever get.

Now he is nineteen, and soon he will pack up his stuff, and he and his brother will carry it to the car, and make three trips at least, and his mother will be cheerful and efficient and then weep by the fireplace, and I will be helpful and pay for gas and slip a hundred bucks cash in his jacket, but just as he starts the car, look, there he is on the changing table again! and there he is on the basketball court, drifting intelligently away from his lazy defender into the corner to be open for a lasered pass from his brother the point guard and I am moaning with pleasure at his subtlety in the rickety stands! and here he is coming home from kindergarten *without his shirt*, who loses a shirt at school and merrily spends the day shirtless?

We hardly ever talk about the ravenous of sentences. When I write a sentence there is no time and I am not creaky and my children are small and hilarious and tall and surly and sneering and grinning and shouldering and burling each other in the kitchen and laughing so hard at some wry remark that their stomachs and cheeks hurt for the rest of the day and their father thinks he knows where heaven is, right in the kitchen, who would have thought heaven had sad warped cupboard doors that don't close properly and have been repaired with duct tape and even once with chewing gum don't tell your mother?

Our children were the best things that ever happened to me, and I have known wild passionate romantic love and still astoundingly do, and I have been blessed a thousandfold by generous friends, and I have been granted work I loved and which mattered in the world, and no man ever loved the liquid sinuous quicksilver verb of basketball more than me, and I had the happiest funniest childhood ever, and I am American which is to be graced and rich beyond measure, and while I am bruised I am not yet broken, aged but not yet dead, and my shaggy brain still works, and I can type fast and try to make sentences that sing and roar and snarl and sob and insist that everything that ever happened is still happening and will happen again no matter what anyone says to the contrary.

Look: here we are at the changing table again. My son looks like the later Orson Welles in a diaper. We peel and clean and powder him and purse our lips and lean down to sing into the holy door of his belly button and it's always this moment and soon I will boil water and a stunning woman will laugh so hard she has to lie down. Soon.

Lost Dog Creek

Our creek rises at the top of a serious little hill to the west and slides all the way down our hillside into the lake below. In the summer it's a trickle and in the winter it's a bigger trickle. Only once that I remember did it get big enough to drown anything, which it did, a beaver, although I think maybe the beaver was hit by a car first, as it was not only bedraggled when we found it but much flatter than your usual beaver. My children and I were going to bury the beaver but by the time we came back to the beaver with beaver-burying implements the beaver was gone. I think maybe it washed down into the lake, which feeds a massive river to the east, which feeds a massive river to the north, which feeds the Pacific Ocean, which is *really* massive.

Some people call the creek Lost Dog Creek because one time a neighbor's two dogs got lost there, but I have little children and they like to name things and they have been naming the creek hand over fist for years. One son calls it Squished Beaver Creek and another son calls it Found Dog Creek and my daughter calls it Not A Creek because most of the time it doesn't have any water in it, which means as she says that most of the time it isn't really a creek at all.

The thing is, though, that when they ask me what I want to name the creek I don't have any words for the names I want to name it. I want to name it the way it mumbles and mutters all day and night in late fall. Or the gargly word it says after a month of rain. Or all the names of the colors it is. Or the deer-language names of the two deer we saw there once. Or the *bip bip bip* sound the deer made when they bounded away like rabbits on steroids. Or the sound of the wheelchair of the guy who lives in the new house above it. Or the sluggish murky sound of people dumping motor oil in it. Or a really *long* name like how long it's been creeking. Or the first words of all the prayers prayed in the tiny wooden prayer shed there, the one that looks like a bus stop for elves. Or the plopping sound chestnuts make when they rain into the creek every fall. Or the sound of the bamboos sucking creek water all day and night like skinny green drunks. Or the whirring song of the water ouzel we saw there once. Or the wet scuttly sound of crawdads running from kids wading or the screechy sound of kids scuttling from crawdads. Or the whinnying of the million robins that live there. Or the name of the first person who drank from the creek twenty thousand years ago. Or the proper word for the prickly pride of the old lady who lives in the basement of the cement house above the creek who says her husband's on vacation but he's actually been gone for ten years. Or the sound that the creek doesn't make when there's no water in it. Or the sound that a kid down the street made right after she learned how to walk and she wobbled all the way down the street holding her mama's pinky and when she teetered past the creek she looked at it amazed and said an amazed word that no one ever said before in the world and maybe no one ever will again and the word fell tumbling end over end into the creek and away it went to the lake and to the river and to the next river and to the ocean where everything goes eventually.

But I bet someday the word will come back. I bet one day a woman will be walking along the creek and when her child asks the name of the creek the mother will open her mouth and inside her will still be the kid down the street she once was and out will come the name of the creek again, salty and wet and amazed.

The Anchoviad

My daughter, age six, sleeps with her bear, also age six. My son, age three, sleeps with his basketball and a stuffed tiger, age unknown. My other son, also age three, sleeps with a can of anchovy fillets—King Oscar brand, caught off Morocco and distributed by the H. J. Nosaki Company in New York. He sleeps with the can every night, won't go to sleep without it under his right cheek. The can is bright red and features a drawing of King Oscar, an avuncular, bearded fellow, apparently a benevolent despot. Every night after Liam is asleep I gently delete the can from his grip and examine it. It's a roll-key can, fifty-six grams, with "about six fillets (15g)." Other than the friendly visage of King Oscar, my favorite thing about the can is the word "about," a rare concession, in the corporate world, to ambiguity. I suppose it's a legal thing, but still it pleases me, for murky reasons.

I sit there in the dark, holding the anchovies, and ponder other murky things like: What's the deal with this boy and his anchovies? How is it that we are drawn to the odd things we love? How came anchovies from Morocco to be swimming headless under my son's cheek in Oregon? What do we know about anchovies other than their savory saltiness? What really do we know well about any creature, including and most of all ourselves, and how is it that even though we know painfully little about anything we often manage world-wrenching hubris about our wisdom?

Consider the six animals in the can. They are members of the family Engraulidae, the anchovies, which range in size from a Brazilian anchovy the size of your thumbnail to a ravenous New Guinea anchovy as long as your forearm. Anchovies don't survive in captivity, and they don't survive long after being netted, either, so we know little about them—but that little is riveting:

- Their hearing is perhaps the sharpest of any marine animal, and the frequency they hear best is, eerily, exactly the frequency of the tail beats of other fish. Is their unimaginably crisp hearing how they manage to swim in darting collectives that twist as one astonishing creature? We don't know.
- Their noses contain a sensory organ that no other creature in the world has. What's it for? No one knows.
- Sensory complexes in anchovies' heads also form dense nets in the cheeks. What do these nets do? A puzzle.
- Anchovies get their food by dragging their open mouths through the ocean in mammoth schools, but what, exactly, do they eat? Surprise: no one knows.

Among the species of anchovy are, to the delight of meditative fathers sitting in the dark on their sons' beds, the buccaneer anchovy (which ranges farthest into the open ocean), and the sabertooth anchovy, which has very large teeth and hangs around, understandably, by itself. And I do not even mention the anchovy's cousin, the wolf herring, which grows to be a yard long and has so many teeth that it has teeth on its *tongue*.

Thus the anchovy, fully as mysterious a creature as, well, as this boy sleeping with the fishes. And what, really, do I know irrefutably about my son? Some of his quirks, a bit of his character, his peculiar dietary habits, the lilt of his song, the ache of his sob, where his scars are, the way his hair wants to go, the knock of his knees—and not much else. He is a startling, one-time-only, bone-headed miracle with a sensory complex in his head and heart that I can only guess at and dimly try to savor in the few brilliant moments I have been given to swim with him. He is a sort of anchovy, as are we all; so I sing our collective salty song—the song of fast, mysterious, open-mouthed creatures, traveling with vast schools of our fellows, listening intently, savoring the least of our brethren, and doing our absolute level best to avoid the wolf herring.

Mammalian Observation Project: Subject J

6:42 a.m. Awakes. Subject is three years old, a twin. Other twin, also resident, still sleeping. J leaves bedding area, smacks twin experimentally, draws moan, pads away happily. Enters maternal bedding area, uses Arctic hand to investigate sleeping mother, who awakens with a shriek.

6:44 Accompanies snarling father into washing area. Father showers while J sits companionably nearby, swinging legs, contemplating mayhem. Flushes toilet several times as father is showering. Roars from scalded father. J flees.

6:49 Father pads back into to bedding area to dress. J returns surreptitiously to washing area, washes Buzz Lightyear action figure thoroughly, including private parts, with soap, using his brother's toothbrush, and fails to turn off tap.

7:13 Mother discovers ocean in bathroom. Chaos and mayhem.

7:25 Father delivers peanut-butter-and-jelly toast, on favorite bread, toasted exactly one minute, cut in quarters, crusts deleted, all presented on favorite chipped Peter Rabbit plate.

7:26 Toast and plate hit floor: Toast *poopy*. Daddy *poopy*. Time out: 3 minutes.

7:31 "StoryTime" television program begins. "StoryTime" *poopy*. Time out: 2 minutes. During penalty phase J strips himself naked, urinates on floor, wakes brother with repeated smacks to the brother's head with a stuffed rabbit, brother wails to be released from room, father releases wailing brother, small naked quick J also escapes. Manhunt begins.

7:36 Manhunt ends when J is found in pantry, where he has also urinated on floor. Time out, 6000 minutes, says snarling father; 5 minutes, says mother. How could a kid possibly have that much urine in his urine tank? It's just not possible. The kid must have a bladder the size of Utah.

7:41 Subject permitted to exit penalty area. Vanishes into outside wilderness.

7:42 Father tracks down subject who is sitting in the yard looking all too pleased. Father moans, knowing what almost certainly happened. Father turns to go in house but instantly turns back, realizing he had better corral subject before further chaos and hubbub, but indeed, at

7:43 Subject has climbed fence into yard next door with the Huge Evil Demon Dog which once ate a Girl Scout. Father shuffles briskly to fence, finds Horrible Terrifying Dog huddled on porch moaning, just totally out of his class crime-wise, and realizing it for the first time, a terrible shock to the dog, poor thing, to have such a powerful concept of yourself, and then realize that there are many quicker relentless mischiefs out there, who knew? Father retrieves subject with series of egregious lies about presents and cookies. Subject pees on neighbor's fence on way back over, apparently as territorial marker. Dog moans again and covers face with paws. Poor thing.

7:45 Father lies egregiously about an early meeting at work that he *cannot* miss no matter what, a *huge* meeting, about, well, something huge, he cannot even say what it's about, it's exactly that huge. Huge, he says. Mother skeptical but, being good at heart, takes over subject wrangling. Father, moved, and not a little gleeful about escaping, decides to leave work early and buy best bottle of wine in universe for mother, but then reflects that probably that's how this all started, if you think about it for a minute. Says goodbye to subject, carefully, from a distance. Subject smiles and waves and as soon as father is out of view says firmly *Daddy poopy.*

Things My Kids Have Said That
They Do Not Know I Know They Said

How come the only things that get made into sandwiches are animals and vegetables? Why don't we have mineral sandwiches, if minerals are so good for you?

If you really like Jell-O, and you really like mayonnaise, then you should be able to *have* a Jell-O and mayonnaise sandwich, and Dad is *wrong*.

One of our grandfathers is dead, and now he is in a cemetery growing flowers.

The reason the ocean is salty is because all the animals in it have been peeing *right in it* since before there was even such a thing as *time*.

Dad says all beings are holy in the same proportions, except the Los Angeles Lakers, who are creatures of the devil.

If ducks married geese, would they make deese or gucks?

Dad says the only reason people are not allowed to marry animals yet is because filing joint tax returns would be too complicated.

A shrew is like a mouse with a bad temper.

The best way to eat a worm is to have another kid do it.

Dad says people are arrogant about being smarter than animals because we have opposable thumbs but look what we messed up with our opposable thumbs.

Insects rule the world but they don't bother talking about it.

The way to tell a mammal from an amphibian is snot.

If you shake hands with an evergreen tree and the branch bites your hand, that's a spruce.

Mom says camping is a way to see God up close but Dad says God loves us and wants us to shower daily.

If you find poop in the woods and it's tiny round balls, it's a rabbit. If the balls are larger it is a deer or elk. If they are *really* large you should come home.

Eagles can see so well they can see what you did *yesterday*.

Dad says people still kill whales for money even though whales have languages and songs and ways to talk to each other miles away that we don't understand, but he must be teasing. Who would kill something who could teach you something you couldn't imagine?

Plants are smart because they can eat sunlight and minerals and we can't, yet.

Dad says every time you go for a walk in the woods you ought to get credit for a week of college.

Mom says polluting the land is a crime but ruining the ocean is a sin.

Some trees can drink *clouds*. Is that cool or what?

Best Napper of the Year

On my second day of kindergarten, at a school named for a species of tree, I discovered that our teacher, Miss Appleby, presented a Best Napper Award every week, and the child who earned the most weekly napping awards was then presented with the Best Napper of the Year Award in June, on the last day of school, in assembly, before the entire school, which went from kindergarten to sixth grade, and contained some two hundred students, none of whom, I determined immediately, would outnap *me*.

I report with admirable modesty that I won the first week's Best Napper Award, defeating Michael A., who slept like a rock but flung his feet and fists as he slept (he had six brothers at home). I also won Week Two, in a landslide, but a small moist boy named Brian F. beat me in Week Three, and battle was joined.

We were *all* small, relatively—I mean, this was kindergarten—but Brian F. was especially small; my older brother Kevin, who came to get me one day after school and got a close look at Brian F., said he looked like a wizened pocket gopher—and I felt his size gave him an advantage, in that he could get down faster to his napping mat and was less likely to be kicked or jostled than someone, say, my size. I appealed to Miss Appleby, on the advice of my brother Kevin, who said I should ask for a point system or a staggered start, but she ruled that Brian F. did not have significant or substantive advantage, and we went on to Week Four.

It is interesting to note here, by the way, that the girls in our class were terrible nappers; I think a girl won the award only three times in thirty weeks, and one of those awards was tainted, I felt, as both Brian F. and I were out sick that week. The winner that week was Margaret O'S., who couldn't nap if you gave her a cot and a pillow and a quart of gin. My brother Kevin advised me to appeal the award that week but our dad said no, using the word *litigiousness*, which I had never heard before.

Mostly it was Brian F. and me trading awards all through the fall and into winter, although I remember a boy named Michael C. stole the last one before Christmas, by egregiously faking his nap, as another boy proved by kicking Michael C. in the ribs, but Miss Appleby did not notice, or pretended not to notice; the fact is that Miss Appleby was a sly woman, and often pretended not to notice things that no person with eyes and ears could fail to notice, like Margaret O'S. being a simpering devious sycophant who sucked up to Miss Appleby in the most shocking fashion so as to win Helper of the Week Award and gold stars for her drawings of cats and New York Yankees and other satanic works. My brother Kevin just last year told me that he saw a news item on Margaret O'S. from which the word *probation* leapt out, to no one's surprise.

During the Christmas break I worked hard on napping and when school started again in January I went on a tear that I think even now must be the record, or close to the record, for consecutive napping awards in that school. I swept, or slept, right through February before Brian F. recovered his game and went on a little run of his own, and we opened April tied at seven awards each. With twelve weeks left in the napping season we were alone at the top, a situation which perhaps rattled us both, as neither of us won the award that month, losing to, in order, Marisa P., who had a cold and was heavily drugged by her mother; Michael A., whose brothers were away at a grandmother's funeral or something, leaving him home

alone with his dad; a girl named Gail N., who came out of nowhere that week, like one of those rock bands that makes one
unbelievably great song and then never makes a memorable
song ever again, like Question Mark & The Mysterians; and a
girl named Colleen H., who later became a nun in a religious
order that worshipped bundles of sticks shaped like canoes,
according to my brother Kevin.

I won the first two weeks of May, Brian F. won the last
two weeks in nail-biters (by now there was betting among the
boys, although none of us had any money and we had to bet
cookies from our lunches), and with three weeks to go we were
again tied. By now even Miss Appleby was caught up in the
competition, and as June opened she announced that while all
of us could and *should* take advantage of Nap Time, she would
set aside a corner of the classroom for Brian F. and me to go
head to head, as it were—best two of three for the title.

June that year was powerfully hot and sticky, and I remember that we could smell some sort of foul algae stench
from a pond nearby, and that was one of the summers of the
thirteen-year cicada (called, no kidding, *Magicicada*), and the
man who mowed the acres of grass around the school went
into a manic phase and mowed all day every day, so it was
harder than usual to drop off thoroughly when Miss Appleby
gave the signal; plus there were the murmurs and burbles of
the other kids, and the faint sound of betting, and the sickly
wheedle of Margaret O'S. sucking up to Miss Appleby, and the
weird feeling of being within a few inches of Brian F., who was
so moist a child that he sweated aloud, and emitted a cloud
of humidity so dense that it was a wonder he was not covered
with moss and lichen and small ferns.

But if the good sweet Lord ever gave me a gift it is the ability
to nap at the drop of a hat, and to sleep soundly until roused

by gentle mom or loving bride, or by a brother with a fist like the knob of a shillelagh, or by a large dog with truly horrifying breath from recently eating a mole, and I report, again with admirable modesty, that I napped Brian F. into the *ground* over the last three weeks of the season, and I won the Best Napper Award for June and for the Year, and had to stand before the entire school assembly on the last day of school, in the gym, with the older kids laughing their heads off at me for reasons I did not understand then and spurn happily now. In my view, setting high standards for yourself is a good thing, and working toward your goal with all your might is a good thing, and how many people can say that they won the Best Napper Award not for a week, like that smarmy insipid Margaret O'S., or two, like poor twitchy Michael A., but for a whole *year*? Not so many, I say, with enviable modesty. Not so many.

The Brilliant Floor

There was a girl named Linda in my first-grade class at Saint John Vianney School in New York. She was shy and tall. She sat in front of me in the first row. We sat in alphabetical order, so that Accopardo was first seat first row and Wyzkyski was fifth row last seat. It was easiest that way for Sister Marie. She was also shy and tall. She was calm and tender and firm and maybe twenty years old. Most of us were six years old but four of us were five. Linda and I were among the fives. The sixes looked down on us as soon as they discovered we were five. They discovered this within the first week of school, and after that there were the sixes and then there were the fives. Why that should matter is a puzzle, but it did.

One day, after a particularly turbulent recess in the playground during which all four of the fives had suffered some indignity from the sixes, we trooped back into our classroom. In Sister Marie's class you were expected to carry the detritus of your lunch back to your desk, so that she could be sure that you had indeed taken sustenance; but this day Sister noticed that Linda's lunchbox was empty. No sandwich wrapper, no cookie crumbs, no apple core. Sister inquired; Linda sat mute. Sister pressed, gently, leaning down to Linda at her tiny desk; Linda covered her face with her hands and wept. Sister realized that Linda had been robbed of her lunch by the sixes, and had not eaten at all, and had been humiliated by the theft, and was more humiliated now by public revelation, and Sister straightened up and stared at each of the sixes, her face unreadable, but just as she began to speak, Linda sobbed even harder, and a rill of urine trickled from the back of her seat and pooled on the floor between the first and second rows.

For a moment there was a ruckus as some children shouted and leapt away from the pool but then Sister said *Silence! Seats!* very firmly indeed—not shouting, but so firmly that everyone sat down in silence—and then she appointed Meghan to lead Linda to the girls' room and then to the school nurse. Meghan held out her arm just like a gentleman does in old movies and Linda took her arm and they stepped over the puddle and left the room. You could hear Linda sobbing all the way down the hall.

The best reason we have schools, I think, is to learn things for which we do not have words or equations. All teachers admit that their students will remember very little, if anything, of the curriculum they were taught; in the end what teachers really do is offer context, manners of approach, and the subtle suggestion that a cheerful humility before all problems of every sort is the only way toward useful grapple, let alone solution. What teachers really teach, it seems to me, is not a subject, but ways to be; a poor teacher teaches one way, and a fine teacher teaches many, some of which may be, to your amazement and relief, ways for you, the student, to open, to navigate, perhaps to soar.

Sister Marie was a fine teacher. We sat silently for a long moment, after Linda left, and then Sister sent a boy to the boys' room and a girl to the girls' room to get all the paper towels they could carry. They came back with one million paper towels. Sister gave each one of the sixes a handful of towel and they mopped up the puddle, one by one, in alphabetical order, by rows. They did this silently. When they were finished Sister handed each of the remaining fives a handful of towel also, and we also knelt and scrubbed the brilliant floor. No one said a word. The sixes then collected our paper towels and put them in the trash. A little while later Linda and Meghan came back and sat down and we started into arithmetic. I never forgot this lesson, and I would bet that no one there that day ever did either, neither the sixes nor the fives.

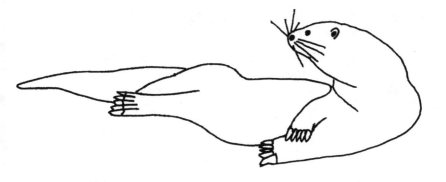

The Killer of Jays

One time when I was a kid in grade school I was out in the seething roaring playground at lunchtime, trying not to get run over by the big kids or accidentally stomp one of the little kids myself, when I found a jay hung by its neck on the fence.

Its head was twisted in a way that heads don't go, and even I, untutored then in physiology and torque, knew that this was death. Its wings were awry and its beak was open and a bit of its tongue had fallen out of its mouth. The tongue was such a deep dark red that it looked black. The jay hung on the fence just at my eye level, about four feet high. The fence divided the school playground from a neighbor's yard and the neighbor was the kind of neighbor who never returned balls if they went over his fence. You had to climb over the fence terrified and drop down from the top after hanging by your hands for an instant. The weakest and littlest among us were sent to retrieve balls from that neighbor. He didn't have a dog but he would yell if he saw someone in his yard and then he would complain to the school and we would be grilled and given detention the next day after someone had retrieved a ball. We wondered if he sat in his window all day waiting for small children to drop into his yard so he could yell and call the school. Maybe that was his job, we thought, yelling and calling the school. Old people had all sorts of odd jobs, we thought, and maybe that's what the neighbor did for a living.

Or maybe he was a killer of jays. Maybe the jays stole fruit from his fruit trees or dug up his garden and ate the seeds and starts. We talked about this among ourselves that afternoon, after all the other schoolkids had come over to stare at the dead jay. The jay had been hung with a piece of thin wire just like the wire you buy at the garden store. Our parents had all bought wire like that for their gardens of tomatoes and beans and radishes. The neighbor had a garden with tomatoes and beans and radishes. Maybe his job was not yelling and calling the school but assassinating jays for people. Maybe he was a professional killer of jays and that was how he made his living. We talked about this for a while there by the fence. Some kids thought we ought to bury the jay and some kids thought we should go tell Sister Marie. One kid said what if we complain and then the neighbor has to go to detention, wouldn't that be great? Another kid said we should take the jay down and throw it around like a football. Another kid said that whoever killed the jay had committed a sin because murdering an innocent being is a sin and killing animals is only allowed when you are going to eat them and no one was going to eat a jay.

Just when we had decided that a committee should go tell Sister Marie about how the neighbor was a killer of jays, a big kid came over and laughed at us stupid kids and said he had strangled the jay with his bare hands and hung it on the fence with a piece of wire he found in the schoolyard. He said it had a broken wing and couldn't get away and it was a mercy killing and then he laughed and ran off. One kid said quietly that's a lie and that's not a mercy killing. A few minutes after that the bell rang and we had to go back to class and I remember the jay was still hanging there like a blue splash on the fence. That night when I got home I tried to tell my mom about the way the jay sagged from the wire around its neck and I cried and couldn't finish the story. I didn't know why I was crying so hard but my mom did. The next day when we went back out in the schoolyard the jay was gone. The janitor told Sister Marie later that he had gently taken it down from the fence and folded it back together the way it had been before it was killed and then he buried it in a shoebox in the convent garden. He told Sister Marie that he had wanted to pray at the burial but he didn't know any prayers for jays and she said the very fact that you wanted to pray was exactly the right prayer for that poor creature, John.

Maschinenpistole

And while we are on the subject of summer camps allow me to sing my experience in Boy Scout Camp in the deep forests of the Adirondack Mountains of New York State, long years ago but still fresh to my memory, for not only did we do the usual Scoutish things like build triangular campfires from beech logs, and whittle arrows, and race rickety canoes, but we also stole a camp truck filled with cakes and pies for the other troops' dessert, and slipped out of camp to an amazing nearby diner, and found the rusted shards of what one member of our patrol later ascertained to be a Maschinenpistole used by the Nazi Fallschirmjäger, or paratroopers, in the Second World War.

All these years after we found that scatter of rusted brooding shards of metal in moist shivering ground at the edge of a spruce swamp I wonder how it got from the war over there to the forest here, and who carried it from one haunted wood to another, and why it was smashed to pieces apparently with a ball-peen hammer, and how long it had been moldering there in the swamp, and what had happened to the man or woman or child who smashed it to bits, and who would have eventually discovered it a century or a millennium later, a curious child or an archeology team, and what they would have thought it to be — a shattered religious object, a broken toy, an instrument for some unimaginable music?

If this was a sensible and reasonable essay I would now explain the theft of the dessert truck, and how we waylaid the driver, a Star Scout, and borrowed the truck long enough to heroically deliver forty cakes and pies to our camp, and then return the truck to the spot where he had left it when he courageously leapt to the aid of ostensibly injured fellow

Scouts; and I would briefly and entertainingly report how we plotted a journey through the moonless swamp to the extraordinary diner where the special was roast turkey with mashed potatoes and gravy; and I might mention odd and riveting moments like the time a boy in my patrol fired a whittled arrow at a hawk and the hawk spun in the air like a dancer and dove on the boy who I believe would have lost an ear had he not himself dove into a tent; but no, I return to the Maschinenpistole, for several reasons.

For one thing several of us discovered it at once, so none could claim ownership or primacy, which was rare; for another we all could tell, just staring at it, that it reeked of death, in a cold metallic way that only human beings would inflict on a throbbing green world. And the way we crouched over it together, fascinated and frightened, as we all are, by anything evil; and how we stayed there long, unable to joke about it, but unable also to easily walk away and leave it as a grim shrine, or to bury it for good, and return it to the earth from which it had been forged by men who so wanted a world of gaunt slaves.

If this was fiction or a poem there might be a passage here where we Scouts walked away silently, each boy thinking about the crime of war, the disease of it, the weird way wars are made of courage and grace and rape and insanity all at once; perhaps it would also be dusk, the darkness sifting into the story on little metaphorical feet; but this is a true tale, and we each walked away thinking that we would come back before camp ended and take a piece of the gun as a souvenir, and not tell the other guys; but none of us did that, as I discovered years later. Last year I met all those boys again, now large men, at the wedding of one of our sons, and at the reception we talked hesitantly about the Maschinenpistole, and one by one we admitted that we were still rattled by it, and remembered the feeling of discovering, a few inches from your face, an evil thing, a thing designed brilliantly and specifically for killing men. As the father of the groom said, *all our genius, and this is what we do with it?*

My Salt Farm

I read Elwyn Brooks White's three lean sweet sad novels starting at age twelve, but I did not encounter his extraordinary essays for the first time until I was fifteen, at which point a subtle teacher gave me *One Man's Meat*. I was instantly entranced, read the whole thing in about thirty hours, and decided forthwith to be just like Mr White and have a small farm by the ocean—a "salt farm," as he called his rocky plot, an alluring phrase.

There were some small hurdles. For one thing I was penniless and for another we lived in New York, and I knew my parents well enough to know they would listen gravely and attentively and patiently to my idea for a farm before laughing so hard that my father would be afflicted with catarrh and my mother would drop her cigarette into her raspberry tea. Also I was already a basketball maniac, so I needed to find a way to run the farm between the prison sentence of school and the joys of preparing for my professional basketball career. My solution, I still think, was deft: I would reduce the *scale* of the farm, and entice one of my younger brothers to run it for me as a sharecropper.

The Coherent Mercy, as my parents called the imaginative force that dreamed the universe into being, had thoughtfully provided me with a fleet of younger brothers, and I chose my workforce with care: the youngest, Thomas. He was a sturdy boy, and could handle the heavy work of construction; he was a cheerful and amenable soul, happy to run with scissors or steal from the collection basket at Mass if so instructed by an older brother; and he had a wonderful concentrative capacity—you never saw a boy who could spend so many hours prying the shingles off the garage roof while meticulously saving the gleaming nails with which Dad had affixed them to the roof last summer. So my brother Thomas it was, and we, or rather Thomas, set to work.

Unlike Mr. White we did not have pigs and chickens and geese and such—we did not even have a dog anymore, after little Tippy dug under the neighbor's fence and impregnated the Great Dane, almost certainly using a ladder, as Dad said— so we used insects. We, or rather Thomas, under my direction, marked out tiny fields and pastures, and built tiny walls and dikes, and stole tiny green houses from our sister's Monopoly set, and even laid in a tiny pond, using Dad's shot glass, which he wasn't using just then because of the catarrh.

We, or rather Thomas, then recruited livestock, and here is where matters grew interesting and difficult. The easiest to collect were pill bugs and beetles, but ants were hopelessly nomadic, grasshoppers and crickets were flighty, and bumblebees, despite the fact that they looked like Burl Ives on Gay Pride Parade Day, kept stinging Thomas no matter how many times I told him to be careful and hold them by the middle.

We, or rather Thomas, tried glass ceilings, but Mom wanted her bowls back so she could make that twig-and-beetle casserole she made every Friday, and we tried vinyl, because the Kingston Trio were heinous caterwaulers, and we tried cloth, but our sister took her raincoat back, and finally we quit the ranch altogether. For a little while we tried agriculture, even planting nickels one day, but that did not pan out either, and by then Thomas was growing weary of the labor. To this day I think he exaggerated his academic workload—I mean, *spend an hour with the letter B*, how demanding is that, a *child* could get by in kindergarten—but right about then our mom decided to start what she called a kitchen garden, although as far as we could tell the way a kitchen garden worked was that we, or rather Thomas, dug fish heads and tails *into* the garden and nothing ever came back up out of the dirt, except, sometimes, a nickel.

How to Start Your Kitchen Garden

Whereas we have three children, and they eat like teenagers, being teenagers, we figured we should take advantage of Oregon, where you can drop a seed by accident and have a crop by noon, so we laid out a garden, and planted tomatoes and beans and garlic, and sat back and waited for noon. Within minutes jays appeared, dug up most of the seeds and starts, ate them with alacrity, jeered at me in their Tom Waits voices, and gave me the feathery finger when I hammered on the window and told them to go mill grubs or whatever it is they do when unemployed. Then came the starlings, who ate the rest of the seeds, left me vulgar notes, and stole a new rake I had just bought, at startling expense. Then came the squirrels, who appeared to be so upset that there were no seeds left that they used my son's baseball bat as a battering ram and nearly stove in the garden shed door before the dog, a sort of house wolf, was released to cause havoc and save the gardening implements in their shining ranks, untouched as yet by anyone except the cashier at the store. Then came the slugs and snails, mopping up last shreds, and mammoth raccoons the size of Rick Perry, who used vituperative language and relieved themselves on my gardening gloves, and finally we were visited by two deer, who were so disappointed that we left ten dollars for them in an envelope with a drawing of deer on it.

Things went downhill after that. I tried every seed imaginable. I tried fences. I tried wooden walls. I tried stone walls. I tried walls sprayed with noxious substances. I tried scarecrows. I was going to try sleeping outside in a cot next to the garden with a butter knife and a Metallica tape but was overruled and confined to barracks. I tried leaving the window four inches open and coaxing the house wolf to sleep under the window so that he, with his incredible hearing, might stick his nose out the window at trespassers and utter those terrifying sounds he makes which certainly must mean *I will eat you so fast there will be nothing left but your footprints*, but he declined. I was going to try to grow Venus flytraps and other violent exotica but was overruled. I did once in a fit of pique plant black locust trees but to my astonishment something ate them one night and was violently sick near the recycling bin. In another fit of pique I was planning to plant bricks and paving stones but was overruled and forbidden to use garden implements for one lunar month.

I tried planting plants that were so close to flowering and fruiting you could smell their perfume and almost hear their yearning for a committed and stable relationship. In yet another fit of pique I planted broccoli and asparagus spears purchased from the grocery produce section, first coating the bottoms of their stalks with growth hormone, and this, I must say, seemed like a promising direction, for what animal could possibly eat a broccoli stalk as thick as my wrist, with crown the size of a baby's head? But how wrong I was, for the entire planting was gone in the morning, the garden scattered with little polite thank-you notes, unsigned.

A man can only take so much disappointment, and there were summers there when my spirits sagged like a teenager's pants, but then I was vouchsafed a vision—pole beans! *My* idea for the pole beans was to erect poles twenty times taller than the house, not even eagles were going to get those beans, but I was overruled on that, and the extant poles, and very excellent poles they are, are eight feet high, and covered in season by a dense thicket of pole beans, more than anyone could count. It may be that suburban animals dislike pole beans, or that the beans are able to defend themselves in subtle and telling ways, perhaps with infinitesimal pocketknives or Yoko Ono songs. But this is a matter for serious gardeners, not for amateurs like me.

Melting a Car

Recently a friend of mine took me into the woods near his house on the coast to see his grandfather's car, which used to be a Ford. It has been parked in a swamp in the spruce woods for more than ninety years. You could tell it used to be a car from the bone structure there beneath the riotous blackberry, but that's about all you could say with confidence. My grandfather parked it there, said my friend, and he instructed my dad never to move it, and to instruct all further generations never to move it either, on the theory that eventually it would melt back into the earth from which it had come, which would be a good thing all around, because he hated that car with a deep and abiding hate, and he claimed it was cursed and haunted and filled with bile and spite, and cars in general were implements of destruction, and spoor of the imminent apocalypse, and the veritable and brooding spawn of evil, and other phrases like that. He didn't like trucks either. He was a preacher.

We stared at the car for a while. It was completely covered with blackberry brambles, some as thick as my wrist, and there were young alder trees shouldering either side of it, and a dense mat of skunk cabbage underfoot.

My friend is a chemistry buff and I asked him to explain how exactly a car would melt back into the earth from which it had come.

Well, he said cheerfully, the iron and steel are rusting at a fairly rapid rate, all things considered, as we get around a hundred inches of rain here, and no metal can ultimately survive the rain. Once rust gets a good hold the metal will dissolve. It'll take thousands of years, but it will happen. Mark

my words. Interestingly birds help in this because when they
relieve themselves on the car an acid in their excrement eats
through the paint and exposes the metal and the rust comes
running. The wood and cloth and leather have pretty much
all rotted and dissolved. The rubber mostly deteriorates by
cracking and calving, for which our climate is not ideal—we
hardly ever get freezes or high heat here, which damage rubber
better than a temperate rain forest does. But the rubber will
die eventually. Hundreds of years, maybe more. The one thing
that might last a really long time is the glass. If the windshield
doesn't shatter it might last thousands of years. But I wouldn't
bet on it. A tree falls, an ice storm, a teenager with an attitude,
a bear with a foul temper, a grouse with a bad compass. And
glass is essentially quartz crystals, you know, so eventually they
would abrade and again become sand.

So five thousand years from now maybe this car is utterly
gone?

Yup, said my friend. Probably all that you would see is a
small leafy hill dense with plants. The tree succession here is
alder, spruce, hemlock, so I would guess that where my grandfather parked the spawn of evil there would be a thicket of big
hemlock. They get really big, too. The old guys here tell stories
of hemlock so big people lived in the stumps like cottages.

I stared at the car for a while again while my friend went off
on a long monologue about a cedar tree near here that was so
big it had hemlocks growing *in* it, and how really big trees here
have *thousands* of animals living in them, and how the biggest
trees here are so draped by fog all the time that they figured out
a way to *drink* the fog, which is why such unbelievably big trees
are often found on such piss-poor soil for trees, and how there
are an awful lot of old cars and trucks sprawled and moldering
deep in the woods, you wouldn't *believe* the remote places you

find abandoned cars, the ravines and peaks and such, you have to wonder how in heaven's name the car even *got* there so as to be abandoned, like for example there's reportedly an old car on one of the naked rocks out in the ocean past the sea lion cove, an old fisherman told him one time he took a boat out at neap tide and climbed the rock and discovered that the car was actually *staked and chained* to the rock like Prometheus or whatever, is that weird or what, makes you wonder what exactly went on *there,* you know, people write whole novels about stuff like that, the guy who did that must have really hated that car, and it *had* to have been a guy, you know, only a guy would go to all the trouble to punish a car like that, like my grandfather driving his car into the swamp, and while certainly my grandfather's car has lasted longer than my grandfather, who is also now melting back into the earth, in the end my grandfather's plan for the car and the patient rain will win, which is pretty cool, all things considered, don't you think?

Unfishing

Having never fished for trout nor salmon nor steelhead in Oregon, someday I have to fish for trout or salmon or steelhead, mostly because I have children, and it is a poor and doofus dad who does not at least once or twice take his kids fishing, which I never have and really should, although I take credit for *thinking* about fishing, which is perhaps fishing in the vaguest sense, and I *did* once catch a trout in Vermont, and I did once catch a sunfish in the Atlantic Ocean, though to be fair it was sunning or dead, because my friend and I just hove alongside and picked it up out of the water like you would pick up a piece of wood, which it, the sunfish, rather resembled, activity-wise.

And I did once catch a small mean bluefish on the shore of Plum Island in Massachusetts by falling on it as it flapped on the beach after chasing smaller fish to shore. It bit me with those wild teeth and I thought about biting it back but didn't. I did catch minnows and carp in green still New York ponds. I did catch a sea robin off a dock at Jones Beach, the ugliest fish I ever saw. My large younger brother who is a fisherman and was busy hauling in flounder for dinner stared at me for a while as I stared at the sea robin until I threw the sea robin back. I did once see a huge steelhead in a sea creek get chased out of its pool back into the ocean by a small boy with jelly in his hair. I have seen a huge nearly dead fungused chinook slowly swimming backward in the McKenzie River here in Oregon and reached down and touched it with my hand, which was a remarkable feeling. I do know a man who catches striped bass by fishing off tugboats and ferries in New York Harbor. I do know a man who when he hooks a large fish jumps into the creek or river and runs after it. I did once fish with a silent friend and neither of us said a word from six in the morning until four in the afternoon when my friend asked me quietly to hand him a beer. I did once watch this man gently break the neck of a striped bass and whisper a prayer for its salty soul.

However I remain no fisherman at all, myself, and at age fifty the chances begin to recede for me to ever become a fisherman, but when it comes to fishing I do possess one lovely glorious fishing memory, the sort of memory every man should have, though not the sort of memory most fishermen have, theirs being brave battles with fish and such, whereas mine is catching a single small trout from a canoe in a lake in Vermont and paddling back to shore where a man in a white cook's outfit awaits me. His name is Bob and he is the cook and jack of all trades for the private thousand-acre wilderness preserve and lake and lodge where I am a guest of the man who has the second-largest car dealership in New England, my friend Cam, who once broke both wrists in a ski race and kept racing anyway because the winner received a whole keg of beer, and he won. Anyway Bob the cook says to me politely when I land how would you like your trout today sir? And I say I think we should go baked today, Bob, and he says very good, sir, and I say thank you, Bob, and he says I will have your whiskey sent to the reading room, sir, and I say thank you, Bob, and he takes the small trout from me and I repair to the reading room where I read Roderick Haig-Brown for a while before my whiskey arrives on a silver platter carried by a young woman who will not stay the whole summer with Bob, who has sort of a rotating girlfriend program as far as Cam and I can tell. The trout arrived a few minutes later, baked with rice and almonds, with a delicious salad on the side, and a bottle of excellent red wine from Spain. My lovely bride, who is tiny but sinewy and who has been fly-fishing for trout in streams so deep in the mountains of Idaho that you have to ride horses for a long time to get there, sneers at my trout story and says it's not really fishing at *all*, it's more like grocery shopping or plucking fish from a tank in the front of a restaurant, and anyway I wasn't more than a hundred yards into the lake, but I don't see where any of these objections applies to my fishing story, and that little trout tasted wonderful baked with rice and almonds. My friend Cam tells me that Bob is not the cook anymore at the lodge because one summer he had not one or two but three girlfriends in succession and the third one hit him with an oar after which the members of the lodge decided Bob should transition into auto sales, which he did, and today he is a member of the million-dollar sales club, which is certainly something to be.

The Greatest Nature Essay Ever

Would begin with an image so startling and lovely and wondrous that you would stop riffling through the rest of the mail, take your jacket off, sit down at the table, adjust your spectacles, tell the dog to lie *down*, tell the kids to make their *own* sandwiches for heavenssake, that's why god gave you *hands*, and read straight through the piece, marveling that you had indeed seen or smelled or heard *exactly* that, but never quite articulated it that way, or seen or heard it articulated that way, and you think, *man, this is why I read nature essays, to be startled and moved like that, wow.*

The next two paragraphs would smoothly and gently move you into a story, seemingly a small story, a light tale, easily accessed, something personal but not self-indulgent or self-absorbed on the writer's part, just sort of a cheerful nutty everyday story maybe starring an elk or a mink or a child, but then there would suddenly be a sharp sentence where the dagger enters your heart and the essay spins on a dime like a skater, and you are plunged into *way* deeper water, you didn't see it coming at *all*, and you actually shiver, your whole body shimmers in response to a dart to the heart, which much later, maybe when you are in bed with someone you love and you are trying to evade his or her icy feet, you think, *my god, stories do have roaring power, stories are the most crucial and necessary food, how come we never hardly say that out loud?*

The next three paragraphs then walk inexorably toward a line of explosive conclusions on the horizon like inky alps. Probably the sentences get shorter, more staccato. Terser. Blunter. Shards of sentences. But there's no opinion or commentary, just one line fitting into another, each one making plain inarguable sense, a goat or even a senator could easily understand the sentences and their implications, and there's no shouting, no persuasion, no eloquent dancing and pirouetting, no pronouncements and accusations, no sermons or homilies, just calm clean clear statements one after another, fitting together like people holding hands.

Then an odd paragraph, it almost seems out of place, for half a second you wonder where was the editor? because it appears to be simply a parade of questions, a jumble or pile of them poured out on the page, but as you pick each one up and ponder it you realize they are the sort of questions the late genius poet William Stafford had stacks of in his study, not questions with answers, necessarily, but questions that make you think, questions that are koans, questions that question exactly how sure you are about such and such, which turns out to be more sure than you probably should be, which not-being-quite-sureness, it turns out, is a good thing, and maybe the sign of a mind being opened, not to get all cute and metaphorical or anything.

Then *another* odd paragraph, this is a most unusual and peculiar essay, for right here where you would normally expect some Conclusions, some Advice, some stern Instructions & Directions, there's only the quiet murmur of the writer tiptoeing back to the story he or she was telling you in the second and third paragraphs, the story hoves back into view gently, a little shy, holding its hat, nothing melodramatic, and then it gently slides away off the page and off the stage, it almost evanesces or dissolves, and it's only later after you have read the essay three times with mounting amazement that you see quite how the writer managed the stagecraft there, but that's the stuff of another essay for another time.

And finally the last paragraph. It turns out that the perfect nature essay is quite short, it's a lean taut thing, an arrow and not a cannon, and here at the end there's a flash of humor, and a hint or tone or subtext of sadness, a touch of rue, you can't quite put your finger on it but it's there, a dark thread in the fabric, and there's also a shot of espresso hope, hope against all odds and sense, but rivetingly there's no call to arms, no clarion brassy trumpet blast, no website to which you are directed, no hint that you, yes *you*, should be ashamed of how much water you use or the car you drive or the fact that you just turned the thermostat up to seventy, or that you actually have not voted in the past two elections despite what you told the kids and the goat. Nor is there a rim-shot ending, a bang, a last twist of the dagger. Oddly, sweetly, the essay just ends with a feeling eerily like a warm hand brushed against your cheek, and you sit there, near tears, smiling, and then you stand up. Changed.

What the Air Carries

Question: what weighs five quadrillion tons but you cannot see hide nor hair nor hint of it?

*

Answers: Guilt, responsibility, fatherhood, sorrow, love, history—but here I mean that most crucial of freighted invisibilities, air, the atmosphere, *our* atmosphere, the incredible blanket we breathe, without which our sphere is only another among zillions of lifeless rocks let loose in the endless void. Five quadrillion tons! The parade of zeroes like a circus train behind the engine of the five: 5,000,000,000,000,000 ...

*

It heats and cools, expands and contracts, it is always in motion, and we have spent many thousands of years measuring its motion in words: British sea captain and scientist Sir Francis Beaufort's 1906 scale, which describes winds in lines of terse poetry, from Beaufort Number 1 (*smoke rises vertically*) to 5 (*small trees in leaf begin to sway, crested wavelets form on inland waters*), to 6 (*umbrellas used with difficulty*) to 9 (*chimney pots and slates removed*) to 12 (*devastation*). Or the Smithsonian Institution's 1870 wind scale, citing *a light breeze which sometimes fans the face,* and *a wind that somewhat retards walking,* and *wind that sometimes carries light bodies up into the air.* Or the American physicist Theodore Fujita's 1971 tornado scale, which lists the effects of winds between 113 and 157 miles per hour as *mobile homes demolished, boxcars pushed over, light-object missiles generated,* and for winds between 261 and 318 miles, *trees debarked,* a chilling phrase. Or a 2002 emendation of the Beaufort scale by a wag in Savannah, Georgia, measuring wind power by its effect on lawn furniture: force 11, *lawn furniture airborne,* a riveting phrase.

*

Makes you want to invent your own scale for how air in motion shivers your heart in the prison of your ribs, doesn't it? *Breeze at the beach with sufficient salt to make your eyes water and give you an excuse for the tears that came as you were thinking about your mama's last hours and the way she winked at you right at the end and made you laugh and sob,* or

bracing wind felt upon stepping out the front door of the hospital with new son clamped in your right arm like a moist mewling football, or

wind tart and adamant enough to rattle spectacles in hugely distracting manner while you are down on one knee stammering out a marriage proposal, or

breeze so gentle and insistent and pleasurable that you find yourself grinning and humming for no reason other than you are actually miraculously alive in this bruised and blessed world ...

*

The roaring wondrous vocabulary of the air, all these words for wind, breeze to zephyr ... There is the sirocco, which arises in Africa and blows west to the Atlantic Ocean. There is the chinook, which arises in the Rocky Mountains and blows west to the Pacific Ocean. There is the monsoon, the wind rife with rain, that blows all over the world. In Alaska there are winds called knik, matanuska, pruga, stikine, taku, and williwaw. In Asia and the East there are winds called aajej, arifi, beshabar, datoo, ghibli, haboob, harmattan, imbat, khamsin, nafhat, and simoom. There are typhoons and cyclones, tornados and hurricanes, storms and squalls. There are the Santa Ana winds of California, the desert winds that, noted Raymond Chandler, "curl your hair and make your nerves jump and your skin itch ... meek little wives feel the edge of the carving knife and study their husbands' necks. Anything can happen ..."

*

What the air carries: albatrosses, bullets, currents, dust, electricity, frogs, glances, hawks, hopes, iridescence, jets, kites, loss, moans, neutrons, owls, prayers, quail, regrets, sunlight, titmice, understandings, violence, water, x-rays, yammers, zeppelins.

*

Air is not made of air. It is a composition, a stew, a motley gaggle of gasses. In general, in most cases, wherever you are on this particular rock, the air in which you swim is about eighty percent nitrogen and twenty percent oxygen. There's a little argon (about one percent), and a shred of carbon dioxide, and infinitesimal traces of neon, helium, krypton, hydrogen, xenon, ozone, and radon, but most of what your body slides through and what slides through you is nitrogen, a gas hatched inside stars and mailed to us through the airless void by an unimaginable postal service.

*

A woman I know breathed life back into her infant daughter. The baby stopped breathing and the father sprinted for the phone and authority and emergency and expertise but the mother bent desperately over her baby and locked lips and breathed, the air throbbing through the lungs of these two beings as joined as joined could be, and after a moment the baby's eyes flickered and her lungs staggered awake again and she hauled in the holy air with a convulsive sob. Talk about your resurrections.

*

What the air carries: airs, ballads, curses, darts, effervescence, flying fish, guffaws, hilarity, hissing, irritation, jokes, kingfishers, longing, murmurs, nattering, nighthawks, opinions, passion, quarks, rhythms, sibilance, soil, tittering, ululation, vowels, whispers, xylophone parts flung in utter exasperation, yowls, zest.

*

You can buy air, sell it, rent it, lease it, lend it out, claim it, refuse and deny its use to others. Among nations and urban planners and developers, air is a commodity, a thing measured in footage and mileage and meters. Some air space is greatly coveted—the whirl of wind over what used to be Iraq, the haunted air over what used to be the World Trade Center in New York City. Seven months after the towers were destroyed and the thousands of men and women and children in and among them murdered, two artists and two architects arranged two banks of searchlights nearby and fired two towers of light into the air every night for a month. The lights rose a mile high and could be seen nearly thirty miles away.

*

Question: Why is it that what we need most—air and water—is what we take most for granted?

*

There is air in water. There is air in soil. There is air in ice and in rock. Sometimes air is trapped for millions of years in ice and rock or amber. One study of air trapped in the amber of an extinct pine tree found air bubbles eighty million years old. The scientists who examined the air were startled to discover that it had twice as much oxygen as air does today. Does twice as much available oxygen mean beings can grow twice as large? Does more air explain dinosaurs? If we had twice as much oxygen would we be twice as smart?

*

There is air at the bottom of the sea, inside incalculable

creatures six miles deep, viperfish and dragonfish, fangtooth and loosejaw, eelpout and bobtail. There is air in the bar-headed geese who fly *over* the Himalayas in their business travels. There was a lot of air in the largest flying creature ever, the pterosaur Quetzalcoatlus, three times bigger than your car. There is air in the bee hummingbird, smaller than your thumb. There are some two million species of creature on this sweet earth, and there have been perhaps ten million others, and every one swam in the invisible miracle, and needed it to live, and moved in it with grace and power and zest and thrum. Such a populous and generous thing, air.

*

How was air born? One theory is that sunlight and lightning acted upon water vapor in such a way as to elicit the first gases, on which sunlight and lightning acted to elicit more gases, and the gases acted upon each other in such ways as to allow for living beings made of gas and light and water. The short answer to the question: no one knows. The long answer: there are more things mysterious and miraculous between heaven and earth than we will ever know in a million years.

*

Air is an endangered species, of course. We know this but we ignore it. We nod in agreement when we hear or read or say something chilling and piercing about increasing poison in the air, but we do nothing. We know beyond the shadow of a doubt that cars and furnaces and factories belch poisons into the air, belch poisons into our children, choke plants and ani-mals and birds and those we love, but we do nothing. We know poisons in the air are ferocious volleys of lead fired into us all, as the great Uruguayan writer Eduardo Galeano says, but we do nothing. We issue words in vast webs into the air, opinions and commentaries, white papers and websites, debates and discourse, seminars and symposia, platforms and parameters, transcripts and testimonies, and we do nothing. If ever we all at once stopped fighting about the names of God and the color of money, and beamed our lasered arrowed attentions on clean air and clean water, we could make a new world as clean and brilliant as a baby. But we do nothing.

*

What the air carries: ants, baseballs, currawongs, damselflies, egrets, finches, gazelles, herons, ibis, jackdaws, killdeer, lariats, mutters, macaws, negativity, oaths, poems, queries, recriminations, swallows, thanks, Uruguayan writers, vocabularies, willets, yells, the crooning of zookeepers to the miraculous creatures they love.

*

I was once a basketball player, years ago, when I was young and supple, pliable and quick, and nothing gave me as much joy as floating into the air—which is maybe why I wasn't a very productive basketball player. More than anything I wanted to soar to the rim, inventing a shot along the way, or sail into a play unexpectedly to snare a rebound or block a shot, and you never saw a guy so liable to pump fakes. On the break with the ball, one defender to beat, a quick crossover dribble to mess up the defender's feet and then *bang!* away up into the air where anything and everything was possible, where bodies were verbs, unrooted, closer to the light ...

*

I was asthmatic as a boy. I spent many nights as thirsty for air as a fish is for water, gasping in the dark, trying to stay calm, trying not to call out for my dad. One of my sons is asthmatic. I have spent many nights listening to his lungs. He hauls in the ragged air with a desperation so intense I think my heart will explode. So many of us so hungry for the wild food of the air.

*

The air has no end, atmospherically speaking; no one knows quite where the air ends and airlessness begins, which pleases me for murky reasons. Above the earth is the troposphere, about eleven miles high, and then the stratosphere, about thirty miles high, and then the mesosphere and ionosphere, together more than two hundred miles high, and then what is called the plasmasphere, or hydrogen cloud, which sails off into space for thousands of miles. No one has ever been able to measure officially where it ends and where outer space as we know it begins. Isn't that cool? We think we know so much but we really know so little.

*

The first gasp and gulp of air from an infant in any of the million species on our planet. The last exhalation of those returning to dust and salt and starlight. Gasps of shock and surprise. Laughing so hard you have to bend over and gulp air. The propulsion of air in annoyance and exasperation. The deep gulp you take before plunging under water. The steady throb of breathing in sleep. The whistled exhalation in amazement: *wheeewwww.*

*

Children leaping into pools, surf, sandboxes, puddles, predicaments, puzzles, passions. Swimming through the air windmilling their arms, their hands cupping air like water. I never tire of watching my kids and all kids at the beach, in playgrounds, in games, leaping into the air as easily and un-consciously and lightly as leaves. A man or a woman works at getting into the air, and needs a reason for flight—despair, des-tination, destruction, decoration—whereas a child is at home in the air and will leap off a branch or a bicycle or a bed for no reason whatsoever but sheer mammalian zest. Remember that as a species we are just recently down from the trees, said the late great American writer Peter Matthiessen, and I wonder sometimes if we thirst unconsciously for breezes against our bodies, winds in our teeth, air in our hair.

*

What the air carries: arrows, bees, curlews, ditties, ethereal melodies, flickers, golf balls, hurrahs and huzzahs, ibex, jacaranda petals, kestrels, lances, merlins, noises, olfactory misadventures, paradelles, quivers and shivers, rubaiyats, sonnets, terzanelles, the shudders of udders, villanelles, wails, xenophobic rants, yips, the rumble and grumble of zebras as they bed down for the night.

*

Air in words: "I inhale great draughts of space, the east and west are mine, and the north and the south are mine," says that greatest of American poets Walt Whitman. "Drink the wild air," says Ralph Emerson, our worst essayist and greatest aphorist. "Poetry is the journal of a sea animal living on land, wanting to fly in the air," says Carl Sandburg, a fine poet forgotten. "I just put my feet in the air and move them around," says Fred Astaire, who flew. "This land, this air, this water, this planet, this legacy to our young," said the late quiet Paul Tsongas, son of a Greek immigrant, candidate for President of the United States. Do you think that we will ever listen?

*

A friend of mine who is a musician says that the reason so much popular music is in 4/4 time is because that is the harmony of the heartbeat, we have a natural rhythm, an interior melody, and he estimates that hominids have been making songs to that beat for maybe half a million years, and he further estimates that there have been maybe a hundred billion hominids in these last half million years, and that every one of those hominids, male and female, have hummed and sung and warbled songs aloud to that beat, so that if you estimate that every man and woman and child of every evolutionary stage along the hominid highway has sung a thousand songs, which is a totally reasonable guess, considering that everyone whether they can sing or not sings a song or snatch of song every week, then we arrive at a sextillion songs, based on the beat of the heart, launched into the holy air by our species and its forebears since we took it upon ourselves to totter up on our back legs some years ago, which is pretty cool. My calculations could be off and it could be more like a quattuordecillion songs, but you get the point.

Charlie Darwin's Garden

Erasmus Darwin's grandson, who learned taxidermy from a man who had been a slave in South America, who once collected beetles as a competitive sport, who was better at riding horses and hunting birds than he was at his academic lessons, who deftly evaded becoming a parson by going to sea, and who, when trying to decide if he should ask his cousin to marry him, wrote that one advantage to marriage was that a wife would be a better companion in old age "than a dog, anyhow," once cleared a small plot of land in his orchard and then carefully tracked the germination and growth of everything that landed and sprouted there.

Despite Darwin's results—more than half the wild seedlings vanished as soon as they emerged, Darwin blaming slugs for the devastation—this seemed like an excellent lazy natural history project for my sons and me to conduct, inasmuch as it appeared to require small labor up front and then a lot of cheerful cursing at slugs, which we do anyway, so we cleared a patch of Oregon soil the size of a beach towel and sat back to watch the slow movie of what would be.

First up, no surprise, grasses and sedges—as far as we could tell, bentgrass, and some kind of fescue, we couldn't tell which, partly because there are about ninety species of fescue, and as one son said none of us really wanted to check its genitals, and also because one of us, no names named, sat right *on* it and squashed it, because *someone* pushed him, so it wasn't *his* fault, so everyone got sent to their rooms.

Next up, also no surprise, *Arum italicum*, the Italian arum, or lord-and-ladies, or cuckoo-pint, which isn't native here, and is hated by gardeners because you cannot kill it no matter what poison or mowing or witchcraft you apply, and there is a vast jungle of it by the mailbox, kept in check by the snarling woman of the house with an annual weed-whipping on the borders, which we like to watch from the safety of the porch because you hardly ever see a tiny woman in a hockey mask cursing and roaring like a drunken sailor as shards of arum fall from the sky like a gentle green mist.

Next: what appears to be *Tiarella trifoliate*, foam flower, which is a lovely little thing, and this too disappears within a couple days. I am leaning toward blaming the slugs like Darwin, that whiner, but then one son tells me in confidence the other son took it to a girl named Sophie who kissed him behind the play structure at school when Teacher Anne wasn't watching.

Next: *Limnanthes douglasii*, meadow foam, which sets me off on a disquisition about the great botanist David Douglas, who wandered thousands of miles through the Pacific Northwest, and who wanted to *hike the whole world*, no small ambition there, but he died young, but as one son says, Dad this is *really* boring, so we move on.

Next: good old *Taraxacum*, the dandelion, which might be the most interesting plant in the history of the universe—a plant that makes decent wine, a wild plant even knotheads can identify and eat, a plant beloved of shark moths, leopard moths, nutmeg moths, and satellite moths, a plant that closes up shop at night, a plant that deliberately boxes out neighboring grasses, a plant that might be thirty million years old, the plant of a thousand names, the lion's tooth, the dog piss, the dog milk, the butter flower, the worm rose …

And finally, before we are instructed to close Charlie's Garden because *someone* thinks it's an eyesore and *someone* seems to be in charge of agriculture because *someone* has the weed whipper and the all-important Toronto Maple Leafs helmet, we find *Lactuca biennis*, tall blue lettuce, which is a native of Oregon and isn't lettuce-looking at all, it's a scrawny leggy plant that looks like a praying mantis on steroids with blue flowers popping out of its elbows. I issue a final lecture on Darwin's last years, during which he bent all his creative efforts to plants and worms, and we turn the garden over and plant bush beans and go watch the hockey playoffs. Two weeks later when the seedlings should be up there is nothing but the headless sticks where the slugs have grazed, and I have to laugh and say a prayer for Charlie.

My Land

Fifty by one hundred yards: a "standard lot," a measurement of standardicity tracing back essentially to Thomas Jefferson, who owned a major honking piece of Virginia and probably would have considered my shard of America something on which to build an infinitesimal shed to dismember pigs or stash his many cases of excellent French wine or ogle the estate slaves. But he owned his land, whereas I do not, not really. According to the laws of the United States, my family shares responsibility for "ownership" with our bank, which holds so many mortgages on the house and property they have lost count at the branch office and probably use our financial history as a scary part of training programs for the tall children they appear to be hiring by the thousands despite the ballyhooed economic dismay, which I wonder how that works, that banks that are said to be failing sure seem to be building vast new armies of loan officers, and you wonder what for? Me, personally, I think Canada is finally making the land grab it has secretly contemplated for centuries, and I think Canadians are faking this whole reserved pale dull silent polite Children of the North gig, actually they are rapacious land barons who will build tiny sheds everywhere and dismember pigs and enslave us and then ogle us, but what do I know?

I do know that my land was inundated by floods for thousands of years, floods thought to have been hundreds of feet deep, icy epic floods from Montana, the Bretz or Missoula Floods, which carved the valley where we live, and scoured the rocks, and left uncountable tons of soil behind when they finally ceased, and then for thousands of years, maybe millions, animals wandered across my land, some of them epic and immense animals, like mammoths, and beavers the size of cars, and some animals perhaps never yet discovered by science, which is a cool thought, albeit sad, in that they will never wander through the front yard again and scare the willies out of my children.

Then brown people wandered into the valley and across my land, which may have been inhabited, whereas it sits on the gentle hill over a lake that used to be crammed with salmon the size of your leg, so you could easily shuffle down to the lake to wrestle your dinner to shore but also return to an abode safe from the roaring floods the lake must have been subject to, one of which happened thirteen years ago, which I remember vividly because my daughter, then age four, stood on the porch with me and as we listened to the lake boiling over the tiny dam that had until that evening regulated drainage to a trickling creek to the muscular river nearby, she said *is a lake still a lake if it's moving?* which is an excellent question, and not one I can answer.

Then came whiter people. They were meticulous keepers of financial records, those pale people, and I sit in the county clerk's archives and paw through the story of my land. In 1850 it is surveyed by a man who uses the meanders of the river as a guide to plotting plats. By 1860 it is referred to as Widow Welch's North West Corner. By the turn of the century it is owned by a man referred to simply as Miller, who paid $625 for it. By 1910 it is owned by a married couple named Oren and Cora, who wrote the words *hereditaments & appurtenances* in the deed. By 1916 it is owned by a doctor who acquires it as payment of fee incurred by *necessary family services*, you wonder what *that* meant. By 1919 it is owned by a couple named Adolph and Mary. By 1924 there is a small white wooden house on the land, built by a woman for her daughter as a wedding present. By 1960, my oldest neighbors tell me, the house was so overgrown with blackberry brambles that the men of the neighborhood once cut holes in the brambles for windows and doors, the resident at the time not allowing them to cut the brambles at the roots, because *it would be wrong to kill a living creature*, she is said to have said.

When we bought the land, fifteen years ago, a transaction that still mystifies me, as we had about a hundred dollars at the time, a friend of mine who used to be a logger came and did a timber cruise on the land. I pointed out that this would take about eleven seconds, the lot being fifty by one hundred, but he said no, you ought to meet your neighbors of every kind when you arrive, so he walked me around my land, and he named every single plant and tree and bush, and showed me a scrub jay nest I hadn't noticed. And all these years later I remember what he said to me when he was done. *It's not your land, he said, no matter what the law says. Be kind to it and keep it clean for when you pass it on to the next idiot. It's as holy as you are. Treat it that way.*

To which, you know, the only proper and respectful thing to say is amen. So I say that, here at the end, and I invite you to say it with me. Amen, brothers and sisters! And beware of Canada!

In the Hills of Willamina

A man named Tim tells me a story. He is a farmer in a valley in Oregon.

My family used to own the whole valley, he says, which we got as a land grant from Andrew Johnson, the seventeenth president of the United States, but over the years we had to sell off some parts, so now we own a hundred and thirty acres, mostly up and over this ridge, which we will never sell, my son and daughter have sworn and vowed never to sell. I used to be a lumber broker, but ever since I was a kid I wanted to be a farmer like my dad, so we grew winter wheat for years, but it's a hard crop to sell, I'd have five truckloads of wheat and not break even on the year, so now I lease out a lot of land to fescue, which is grass seed, you know.

Well, you ask me about that car up in the tree there, I'll tell you, that started years ago one Halloween night when a car broke down on the road out front of our house, and the fella driving it came up here knocking, and we went to help, of course, but you could see the car was gone, everything was dead, and the fella, he was headed to the casino, he proposed that if I gave him a ride over to the casino he would give me the car, so we did that. Well, it was Halloween, so we buried the car head down in the dirt out front, like on the Cadillac ranch in Texas, and we got a mannequin and had it falling out the window, and a lady driving by saw that and called the paramedics, and they came rushing out to the house thinking it was a crash.

Well, *they* thought it was funny, but a few minutes later a county mountie rode up, and he did *not* think it was funny, and he says that paramedic call just cost the county eight hundred dollars, which the county would pay, but the next call would be eight hundred bucks coming out of *my* pocket, so we took down the car. But a couple days later some guys were out here putting up telephone poles with an enormous crane and I had an idea and I asked those fellas if they could hoist the car, it's a Studebaker, up into a tree, and they said sure, so they did that, wedged it in good, into a big old oak tree. They charged me a bottle of vodka for the work, a very fair price. Well, that was ten or twelve years ago now, I don't recall exactly, and we have had some storms with winds near a hundred miles high, and that car never budged. That thing is in there for good. People stop by every week or so, sure, to ask about it, just like you. Kids often think it's the flying car from the Harry Potter books, though I don't think that was a Studebaker. Some people ask did we park the car over the tree when it was little and the tree lifted up the car, but I have to tell them no, although it's awful tempting to tell them yes, but the answer's no, we put it there, and it might well be there a hundred years. Last year we got more than a hundred inches of rain here, you know. I bet that car will be up there until it rusts to death, which might take a hundred years or more. Check back in a hundred years and see, why don't you?

The Best Soccer Player in the World ...

... sat at a rickety table the other night, behind the looming south wall of the field on which there is a fifteen-foot-high photograph of herself in her college jersey, and signed autographs for, by my count, two hundred children. The children were mostly girls but there was a startling number of boys and they had the same look on their faces as the girls did, something like anticipation and awe and delight and trepidation and wonder that they were actually no kidding about to shake hands with and be smiled upon by the Best Soccer Player in the World, who looked remarkably like a regular human being, with scruffy sneakers and surfer shorts and a shy smile, despite the fact that she is the Best Soccer Player in the World, and millions of people around the planet had just stared at their screens in amazement as she had the greatest performance in Olympic soccer history, and now she is second all-time in history in goals scored against teams from other countries than her native Canada, and pretty soon she will be first, and this after having one of the greatest college careers in soccer history on the field about a hundred feet from where she sat at the rickety table, signing programs, scraps of paper, a baseball mitt, hats, shirts, two casts (both left arms, oddly), photographs, and a proof-of-insurance card that a dad hurriedly pulled out of his wallet when his daughter was about to burst into tears because she had nothing for Christine Sinclair to sign.

I stood a few feet away from the rickety table for a while and watched the children shuffle closer and closer until they were in the Presence, and a remarkable number of children stood and stared down at their shoes as their moms and dads urged them to at least say hi or *something* after waiting on line for so long for heavenssake, and I have to say that the way most of them then utterly shyly glanced up at the Best Soccer Player in the World and found her grinning gently at them and quietly saying *hey, you excited for the game tonight? you love soccer too, don't you? isn't it the greatest game?* gave me the happy willies, because the children's faces then lit up like lamps! because She was talking to them! and She was friendly and gentle and not officious and cocky and self-absorbed in the least! She's like a regular *person*!

Most of the children then did proffer something to be signed, but more than a few just stood there thrilled and agog as they shook Her hand, and beamed even more as She said something gentle and friendly to them as their moms or dads edged them past the rickety table, because the line must keep moving, there are *lots* of other kids waiting to talk to Her, but I watched a few kids, as they got past the table and were steered toward the field by their moms and dads, stare at their autographed scraps of paper like they were objects beyond any calculation or measurement of value, which they were. One girl who looked about six years old kissed her scrap of paper before she tucked it away carefully in a stunning pink purse.

After about an hour it was time for the Best Soccer Player in the World to wrap up, and the table was dismantled, and She ambled off to watch her alma mater open another season with another victory, but I stayed where I was, watching her wade through a shallow sea of small children who reached up to touch her hands as she passed through them like a tall dream. Then She turned the corner and vanished, and it was time for the game to begin, but you would be surprised how many children stayed right where they were, there in the concourse, even as their moms and dads were chivvying them toward the field. I watched one small girl be expertly herded toward the stands by her dad, who angled himself so she couldn't see the huge candy bars for sale, but just before they entered the tunnel the girl turned and looked back, as if perhaps Christine Sinclair would again magically appear, looking like a regular human person! You wouldn't *believe* that the best soccer player in the world is a regular human person with scruffy sneakers and surfer shorts and a shy smile, but this is so, and She was back on campus the other night, and there are hundreds of children who will never forget the moment that She leaned down and said something gentle and funny to them and shook their hands and looked them in the eye and saw them for the holy astounding shy beings they are.

Some moments, it seems to me, are beyond any calculation or measurement of value. I saw a few, the other night, behind the college soccer field.

A Note on Cricket

I had the startling luck of seeing a game of cricket for the first time at a world shrine of cricket, the Melbourne Cricket Ground, in Australia, and something about the weather in Oregon this balmy afternoon, the crack of baseball bats somewhere in the distance, the gentle breeze with fresh clean green in it, the urge to lie down lazily in the grass and gawk at birds, brings me back to the legendary MCG, for the Queensland v. Victoria match.

I knew nothing about the old game, beloved now in every corner of the former English Empire (could cricket, rugby, ale, and Kipling be the best things that emerged from vast cruel brilliant savage imperial enterprise?), other than it was the father of my home country's game of baseball, so I watched with interest and confusion for a while, until a small boy nearby took pity on me. He ambled up to my row from his seat, perhaps sent by a merciful grandfather.

You are not from here, sir?

Nope—American. Just visiting.

Ah then—you don't know much of cricket?

Nope—I'd like to learn, though.

And a beatific smile spread across his wide wild face; I can see it even now. He was so pleased to be of help, and even more pleased to pour his love for the game into a willing ear. It's a subtle thing, the joy of explaining something you adore to someone who does not know it but is curious and will actually listen, rather than prepare bullet points in riposte. And he poured out his love, his appreciation of small points of positioning and strategy, his wonderful grasp of history and vaunted players (the West Indies' masterful wry Sir Viv Richards! Australia's mad genius Shane Warne! India's unparalleled batsman Sachin Tendulkar!) for an hour, as I sat delighted and overwhelmed; and when finally he went back to his seat, I sat there in the stands of cricket's Yankee Stadium and counted myself blessed; for now I had a loose grasp of how there are *two batsmen at once*, and the "bowler" is the pitcher, and games can technically go on for weeks, and batsmen can technically never be put out, and a "sixer" is a home run, and the players, despite the fact that they look like ice-cream salesmen in their cool shining white First Communion duds, are actually unreal athletes who make astonishing plays in the field with their bare hands, and happily hit the ball sideways and behind them and at odd oblique angles when they are "at stumps," which is to say at bat, and that the way to strike out a batter in this sport is to whip a ball the size and density of a small rock past the batter, to smash against a piece of wood behind him, and produce a stunning roar from the crowd.

But even better than the small knowledge of the game I had been given that day was the memory of that boy, so delighted to share what he loved with all his heart; and even now, when someone who hears me lecturing happily about basketball asks me tartly what is the *point* of sport, is it not a wholesale waste of money and time on useless and unproductive antics, I remember that Australian boy; and I conclude that in the end sport is about love. Yes, it is theater, and yes, it has to do with savoring the astonishing grace and creativity of the human body and mind, and yes, it is about communal pleasure, and yes, it is about beer, and yes, it is about the ancient way we belong to tribes and clans, and delight in our heroic clan, and sneer at the scurrilous others; but in the end it is somehow, beautifully, simply, happily, about love.

My Hero?

That's easy. My dad. And not for the reasons you might think, like he signed up to fight a cruel and rapacious empire even though he thinks violence is a sin; or that he devoted himself to raising his kids rather than be the famous novelist he might have been; or that somehow he never grew bitter and haunted even though four of his eight kids have now, as he says quietly, gone on ahead; or that in sixty years my brothers and sister and I have known the man we can count the number of times he lost his temper on two fingers, which is an average of one meltdown every thirty years, which is terrific average, temper-wise.

Nor is he my hero because his childhood fell apart when he was eight years old and his father lost his job and his sister died and his penniless family lost their house and they took to the road for years all through the heartland until my dad washed up in New York City and diligently built a calm patient intelligent affable gentle self that earned him a free ride through college and the love of my mom.

Nor is he my hero because when he got back from the war in which he and my mom were absolutely sure he was going to die, he joined millions of other veterans who could not find work, and often sat in the park, in his excellent suit and overcoat, trying not to despair, until he found one job and then another, the second of which he did brilliantly for thirty years, serving the stories and grace and brilliance of the Catholic Church he loves to this day despite its greed and cruelty and lies, which are also sins, as he says, but which our collective prayerful work may someday overcome, by the grace of the Mercy.

This is how my dad talks, gently and brilliantly, without any flash and bluster, which is part of the reason he is my hero. His ego is grinning and healthy but small enough to fit in his pocket. His patience and generosity are oceanic. His quiet simple honest grace does not flag nor does it wither. His easy open witty warm humor meets you at the door and pulls a chair out for you and gets you a cup of tea. He knows pain and loss and tragedy and horror and yet he sits there smiling gently and listens carefully and does not issue advice unless you ask politely for it, in which case he issues unbelievably wise advice, which you would be wise to act upon, trust me. He thinks of you before he thinks of himself. This is a rare and lovely flower in the forest of the world. He makes you want to be better. He makes you want to be the best self you could ever be because you want to live up to what he knows you can be. He makes you want to make him proud. You would do anything to make him proud. Trust me. You get down on your knees as often as you can and say to the Mercy o thank you thank you for giving me that man as my dad, o thank you, what a blessing he has been to my mom and my sister and my brothers who are alive and my brothers who have gone on ahead; and to me.

My hero? That's easy. I can answer that question right quick, with alacrity, instantly, without hesitation, without having to think about it, because I have known the answer to that question ever since the moment when I was a teenager when I woke up finally and realized that all I ever wanted to be was half as good a man as my dad. Someday I hope that will happen.

The Thaw

I had been told, upon arriving in Oregon twenty years ago, about the Thaw—a magical week in February, an island in the ocean of winter, when the rains ceased! and the roses bloomed! and the temperature rose sometimes into the seventies! and Oregonians emerged from their holes, blinking and scraping off the moss with special sticks carved from cedar and fir, shaped like magic animals and sandwiches! But it was hard to believe, those first few winters, that this was possible, the silver drumming of the rain being so insistent, the moist ceiling looming day after day, the gray mornings chased by metallic afternoons, week after week, month after pittering plodding precipitous month; but then it happened! And the next year it happened again! And over the years I have learned not only to crave it but to savor it: the sunlight pouring clean and crisp over the steaming earth, the tree frogs roaring, the newts making out furiously in their muddy lovers' lanes, the soggy citizens stumbling out of their homes into their gardens, the first thrum of lawn mowers, the murky thuck of children running across playing fields that look dry but most certainly will not be until probably August for heavenssake but let us not carp and cavil. For a while, in February, a great gift arrives, and it would be a mean and shriveled soul who would complain, perfectly logically and correctly, that the rains will return, washing back over Oregon like vast brooding gray armadas in the sky, until Independence Day—really, has there ever, ever, been a dry Rose Festival? Yes, the tide will rise again after The Thaw, and we will shuffle along mooing in the mist, umbrellas jostling, shoes sloshed, socks soaked, suits splashed, sunglasses bereft and forgotten in a lonely drawer, the dog writing muddy music all over the floor again, until that brief weekend we call high summer here; but for a moment late in winter there is a week of wondrous light that thrills the wet shivering mammal inside each of us, and makes us mumble happily, and write silly essays, and understand why our forebears worshipped the sun, and dig the genius of Easter, which is about brilliance emerging from the long dark, yes? So then, all together now, a salute to the Thaw! and o my god who let the dog in again! Look at his feet! Am I the only one in this blessed family who does not want to have the whole blessed yard in the blessed kitchen bless my blessed soul? Where is the towel? Don't use your shirt! I have already done six hundred loads of laundry this morning alone! Sweet mother of the mewling baby Lord Jesus! Is it ever going to stop raining so we can stumble out of the house and sprawl in the holy grass and moan happily as we steam redolently like fresh loaves of bread? Yes, I am talking to you! Where is the dog?!

The Hawk

Recently a man in my town took up residence on the town football field, in a small tent in the northwestern corner, near the copse of cedars. He had been a terrific football player some years ago for our high school, and then played in college, and then played a couple of years in the nether reaches of the professional ranks, where a man might get paid a hundred bucks a game plus bonuses for touchdowns and sacks, and then he had entered into several business ventures, but these had not gone so well, and he had married and had children, but that had not gone so well either, and finally he took up residence on the football field, because, as he said, that was where things *had* gone well, and while he knew for sure that people thought he was nuts to pitch a tent on the field, he sort of needed to get balanced again, and there was something about the field that was working for him in that way as far as he could tell after a few days, so, with all due respect to people who thought he was a nutcase, he thought he would stay there until someone made him leave. He had already spoken with the cops, he said, and it was a mark of the general decency of our town that he was told he could stay awhile as long as he didn't interfere with use of the field, which of course he would never think of doing such a thing, and it was summer, anyways, so the field wasn't in use much.

He had been nicknamed the Hawk when he was a player, for his habit of lurking around almost lazily on defense and then making a stunning strike, and he still speaks the way he played, quietly but then amazingly, and when we sat on the visiting team's bench the other day he said some quietly amazing things, which I think you should hear.

The reporter from the paper came by the other day, he said, and she wanted to write a story about the failure of the American dream, and the collapse of the social contract, and she was just *melting* to use football as a metaphor for something or other, and I know she was just trying to do her job, but I kept telling her things that didn't fit what she wanted, like that people come by and leave me cookies and sandwiches, and the kids who play lacrosse at night set up a screen so my tent wouldn't get peppered by stray shots, and the cops drift by at night to make sure no one's giving me grief. Everyone gets nailed at some point so we understand someone getting nailed and trying to get back up on his feet again. I am not a drunk and there are no politicians to blame. I just lost my balance. People are good to me. You try to get lined up again. I keep the field clean. Mostly it's discarded water bottles. Lost cell phones I hang in a plastic bag by the gate. I walk the perimeter a lot. I saw coyote pups the other day. I don't have anything smart to say. I don't know what things mean. Things just are what they are. I never sat on the visitors' bench before, did you? Someone leaves coffee for me every morning by the gate. The other day a lady came by with twin infants and she let me hold one while we talked about football. That baby weighed about half of nothing. You couldn't believe a human being could be so tiny, and there were two of him. That reporter, she kept asking me what I had learned, what would I say to her readers if there was one thing to say, and I told her what could possibly be better than standing on a football field holding a brand-new human being the size of a coffee cup, you know what I mean? Everything else is sort of a footnote. If you stay really still at dusk you can see the progression of what's in the sky in order, which is swallows, then swifts, then bats, then owls, then lacrosse balls, and when the lacrosse guys are finished they stop by to say hey and to tell me they are turning off the field lights. Real courteous kids, those kids. If the world to come is going to be run by kids who play lacrosse, I think we are in excellent hands.

Moose Poop

When I first flew for business, many years ago when the world was young, I did not bring home gifts to my family, because I was as yet unadorned by spouse and children.

Then, after the epic miracle of a remarkable woman saying yes! after I stammered a marriage proposal (on my knees, in the sand, by the sea), I began to bring gifts home from my occasional business jaunts—generally chocolate, earrings (*lots* of earrings), or the signature gift of the city in which I had been confined for conference or convention—crab cakes from Baltimore, salt-water taffy from Boston, smoked salmon from Seattle, shards of broken glass from Detroit, worn fifty-dollar bills from Chicago, that sort of thing.

Then we, miraculously, had a daughter, and I brought home acres of odd trinkets and toys—stuffed animals, golden apples, music boxes, bright books with hardly any words, et cetera beyond the memory of man. Anything you can imagine that a father besotted by his first child would buy, I bought without a thought for value, including, God help me, chocolate-covered crickets, smoked kangaroo fillets, and a didgeridoo (which was soon conveniently lost; it turns out that giving a didge to a small child who has no idea how to play it but plays it anyway for hours at a time is *not* a good idea, no matter how good an idea it seemed at point of purchase).

Then suddenly we had twin sons, and now the whole dad-bringing-home-gifts-from-his-trips thing reached its (expensive) apex: autographed sports jerseys, hockey helmets, implements for various sports (including, for a reason I cannot now recall under oath, hurling sticks from Ireland, another *very* poor idea), cowboy boots, surfing gear, dashing sunglasses, ukuleles, and hills—nay, mountains—of cookies. Also every sort of candy manufactured to appeal to just my airport demographic, at that point—the dad who, as he shuffles briskly through the airport in Minneapolis or Vancouver, realizes with horror that he has forgotten to get small thoughtful gifts for the children, and seconds later finds that he has purchased many bags of Moose Poop. I kid you not. I have bought dozens of bags of Moose Poop. I may have passed the hundred-bag mark for Moose Poop. I may be, for all I know, a Valued Moose Poop Customer. You wouldn't think that one man would spend something like five hundred dollars of his hard-earned cash over the years on something called Moose Poop, but I tell you this is so.

Well, my children kept getting older and taller, as children generally do, and now they are in college, and they are not home much, and last week, as I was shuffling briskly through an airport toward the plane that would take me home, and I realized with a start of horror that I had forgotten to get small thoughtful gifts for the children, I realized with a curiously powerful tide of sadness that I did not have to buy gifts, there being no children at home to say things like Dad, Moose Poop *again*? It was a remarkably stunning moment, to be honest with you, and I had to sit down for a minute and try not to weep, right there by the toddler playland. You might not think it would be such a big deal to not buy gifts but I am here to tell you it was a deal bigger than big, to me. I know it seems like a little thing in the big scheme of things but the fact is that like almost everything we savor and cherish in this life it was a moment that had to do with love, with a love so ferocious and vast I cannot come close to finding words for it, and can only say the words Moose Poop one last time here at the end, and hope you know exactly what I mean. I bet you do.

That Chickadee Must Be from Chicago

A dear friend of mine is dying and his wife tells me about their days and nights. It's like he's melting, basically, she says. Every day there's a little less of him than the day before, and as you remember he was a majorly big guy. Now he is not a big guy. Now he's like a tall pencil. But there's not much pain. So that's good. First he lost weight, and then hair, and then eyebrows, and then energy, and now it's sentences. He has a million words in his head but now they wander out on their own rather than march in wry coherent parades like the last fifty years. You remember how pithy he was. No more. Now he'll start a story and then it just sort of shuffles off on its own. He starts out talking about mathematics and ends up with parrots. You have to laugh or else you would just cry all day. *He* laughs, for which you have to give him major credit points. He can still laugh, yes. Thank God for that. I think laughter will be the last thing to go for him because it was the first thing to arrive. You remember his mother said he laughed all the time when he was a baby. Also she said he didn't say a word for his first two years and she and his dad were worried that he *couldn't* talk but he laughed a lot, and I think that's what happening now, he laughs a lot but he doesn't really talk anymore. I get in bed and hold him and sometimes he laughs so quiet you can't hear him laugh but you can *feel* him laugh if you are holding him in bed. So that's good. We spend a lot of time in bed laughing. What else can you do? You might as well laugh. *Go down laughing*, that's our theory. We started out together laughing and that's how we will end up. We laughed our asses off when we were courting. Also he sleeps a lot now but even that's changed, he'll fall asleep in the middle of a story and then he wakes up in the middle of another whole story altogether and neither of us knows what he's talking about. It's like the stories are in charge and he just visits them. We laugh when this happens. You have to laugh. The last sentences he had firm by the scruffs of their necks were mostly about birds. He sure loves birds, especially hawks. I angle him in the bed so he can see out the window and we have all the usual suspects at the feeder plus a resident Cooper's hawk. If I prop him up right in bed he can see the bird feeder, which is basically comedy and drama all day long, the stupid squirrels trying everything they can think of to get around the protective hood on the feeder and falling off like furry vaudeville clowns all day, it's hilarious. *Rocks are smarter than squirrels*, he used to say. And the birds do have a pecking order—the big ones push the little ones around, although we have this one chickadee who we think must carry a switchblade or something, all the bigger birds leave in a hurry when he arrives, he's a tough little brother. One of the last coherent sentences he said to me was *that chickadee must be from Chicago*. The hawk strafes the feeder once in a while, and about a week ago we were lying in bed and I was holding him and we both saw the hawk dive for the feeder and he actually sat up in bed and shouted *noooo!*, which was an amazing burst of energy. God knows where *that* came from. Then he fell back exhausted and we started laughing hysterically and that was the best time we have had in a month. For days after that whenever he was having a hard time or I was getting bleak one of us would say *noooo!*, which would send us both into hysterics. So when you think of him, remember that, okay? That will make you laugh, and that's good. That's good.

A Moment

During the summer after I graduated from college, I sought employment every day in New York City, walking all through Manhattan in my thick gray wool suit, interviewing with publishers, meeting with newspaper editors, and gazing in awe at the imposing offices of the *New Yorker* magazine (then on West Forty-Third Street), an edifice I never ever managed to enter, despite many devious and determined assaults; I even tried to slip up the fire escape one blazing afternoon, in my thick gray wool suit, but the fire escape ended abruptly (and illegally) after three floors, and I had to climb back down and take the train home, sweltering.

My dad still worked in the city then, on Park Avenue, east of the meatpacking district and south of the garment district, and often we would ride the train into the city together in the morning, Dad reading the newspaper and me sleeping so soundly I was often utterly discombobulated when Dad woke me gently and said *we are here* and put his hand on my shoulder gently, which was his way then and now of telling me that he loved me without using many words, a graceful economy of language which he still practices, gently.

We would set off from the house together, my mother kissing each of us at the door, and walk briskly toward the train station, under the towering sweet gums and sugar maples of our street, my dad carrying his briefcase, the two of us clad in suits, my dad in sensible linen or cotton, and me in my thick gray wool, already uncomfortable before we reached the end of our block, where we turned to enter the little woods that lay between our street and the station.

Imagine us, then, many years ago, a quiet man and his silent son, entering a small forest, in New York State, quite early in the morning. There are cardinals and robins and jays awake and about already. The father is wearing a fedora hat, the son bareheaded. As the day promises rain, the father has donned his light summer raincoat, and loaned his son his heavier winter raincoat. A skittering in the underbrush turns out to be squirrels, and not, as the son secretly hoped, foxes. The father, a veteran of the army in war, gauges the time to the minute, calculates that they have eight minutes to achieve the train, and sets the pace accordingly; the son, who loves his father but does not yet know how to say this, and has just in recent years recovered from the sneering rudeness of adolescence, follows his father silently through the woods, staring with affection at the broad beige timber of his father's back. Their raincoats swish and rustle. In the distance you can hear the thrum of cars on the highway between the little forest and the train station, but for a moment here are two men, father and son, walking silently through the woods, dappled by the sunlight, walking to the train. Both are wearing their best shoes. In the woods the dew and rising humidity combine to mist the younger man's spectacles just enough for him to imagine for a second that the beige ripple ahead of him is a deer or a cougar.

In a moment these two men will reach the fringe of the woods, and step out onto the pavement, and make their way to the train, and the city, and the future, but not yet; not yet. We have so many delicious moments in life, and they rush past so hurriedly, in such a mist and blur, that we should pause sometimes, I think, and choose one, and stroll back into it, just for a few minutes, and try not to weep from grief, that it was so soon and thoroughly lost, or from joy, that we *had* such a moment, that it was granted to us alone among all the children who ever were and ever will be; so here I am with my dad, many years ago, entering a small forest, in New York State, quite early in the morning, in our rustling raincoats, silent and happy. As the sun rises higher more birds thrill to it and by the time we near the end of the path it seems to me that you can hear every bird that ever was or ever will be, which is a glorious sound.

Sandy

I want to tell you a story for which I cannot find good words. There is a dog and sunlight in it. My sister is driving the car. The huge ancient dog collapsed. My tall taciturn kid brother is sitting next to me. Our grand-aunt just called, sobbing. She is a bigot. We drive along the beach road. You wouldn't *believe* the light this morning. It is tense when our grand-aunt comes to family dinners because she will say things like the Yankees went to hell when they hired niggers to play the outfield. There are men on the jetties fishing for striped bass. Our grand-aunt is blind. She lives with the dog. He is a great dog who shepherds her expertly from couch to kitchen using his shoulders. Our grand-aunt and her sister keened at our grandfather's wedding to our grandmother. Keening is wailing for the dead in the ancient Irish tradition. Our grandmother never spoke to our grand-aunt or her sister the rest of their lives. How stupid Irish is *that*, says our dad. He is Irish too. The dog's name is Sandy. He is a great dog. We think he does the laundry. Our sister drives slowly and cranes her neck to see the street signs. My kid brother isn't saying much this year. The men on the jetties are also hoping for bluefish. Our grand-aunt says she can tell if people on the radio are niggers or not. When we get to the house we can hear her weeping. She says there are more niggers on the radio at night. The front door is locked so we go around back. The back door is unlocked and we go in and say Aunt Loretta? There are piles of newspapers like you wouldn't believe. Why exactly a blind woman would continue to get the paper is a mystery to me, says our dad. When our grand-aunt comes to family dinners she sits at one end of the table and our dad sits at the other end and grinds his teeth. You can hear him do it if you sit close enough. The dog is sprawled on the kitchen floor. There are dirty dishes piled in the sink so high that if you sneezed there would be a calamity. Our sister knows animals the best and she kneels down and asks Sandy questions and he pants and stares at us in the most friendly fashion. He has the thickest whitest eyebrows you ever saw. Our grand-aunt is sobbing on the couch. She tries to explain things but she is not using any words that we know. Sandy is such a huge dog that when he is all sprawled out helpless like this in the kitchen he takes up most of the floor. One time at dinner our grand-aunt said that the niggers were taking over the government and I bet people in Peru heard our dad grinding his teeth. Our sister stands up and says he's dying and we have to get him to the vet. Our grand-aunt cries harder. Sandy stares at us. I remember there was a long pause right here, while Sandy panted and our grand-aunt cried and we tried to calculate how we were going to get Sandy out of the house and into the car, and then my tall kid brother bent down and picked up the dog as if the dog weighed an ounce, and he straightened up, with his arms full of dying dog, and there was some look on his face that I just cannot find the words for. That's the story I wanted to tell you. There was love and pain and fury on his face but then words run out of gas and all I can say is See his face all twisted and shining in the shadowed kitchen? See? This is the biggest heaviest oldest dog you could imagine and it would have been a miracle of all three of us somehow managed to hoist him up and haul him into the car but somehow my brother lifted him like a feather and now the tears are sliding all silver down his face like a river on rock and I open the door and the light pours in. There should be a *sea* of words for this moment but I cannot find them. On the way home no one spoke but we saw a guy on a jetty haul in a huge fish. Probably it was a striped bass but maybe it was a bluefish. It was one tremendous fish. I want to say it was as big as the dog but it wasn't.

Hypoxia

There are fewer frogs. My kids loved listening to the tree frogs in the little swamp down the hill totally losing their minds at night and singing like inebriated folkies at a free picnic where you didn't even have to bring a bowl of some unidentifiable casserole that almost certainly had eggplant in it although what could conceivably be more horrifying than cold eggplant?

There are fish in the river with cancerous tumors on their heads. My son caught one recently and we stared at it and he burst into tears and he is eight years old and watching a boy eight years old weep from the bottom of his bones because a beautiful stunning creature is twisted and misshapen and diseased is a terrible searing tearing thing. And how do I explain it?

How do I say well, son, creosote is important and fish are not? How do I say that? Because that sure seems to be the case.

There are more osprey than there used to be, though, I tell him. See their nest there on the snag by the softball field? There didn't used to be enough osprey to build one of those herculean nests in that snag even though it's right at the juncture where the river and the lake are connected by the creek, and for an osprey that's like having three major grocery stores within two blocks so you could always be assured there would be excellent fish at least at one of the stores at any one time, and all osprey eat is fish, which is why there are fish bones by the left-field line, see that? If you ever play left on this field do *not* dive for a ball hit up the line or you will end up smelling like your Uncle Stephen and that would be bad.

But then I have to explain that we used to kill eagles and

falcons and hawks and osprey because we sprayed foul evil poison everywhere and we still do.

There are dead places in the ocean. He reads the news. He says Dad, what does *hypoxic* mean? Did we do that? He shows me the illustration in the newspaper. The map shows a hypoxic zone this summer exactly where we go to the beach for the ten greatest days of the whole year, when you can skimboard all day long and watch pelicans and seals and sea lions and whales and cormorants and terns and gulls and you can dig for sandcrabs and there are thimbleberries and salalberries behind the dunes and one time we saved that baby murre, remember that time, Dad? And we named him Mike and the lady from the aquarium said they would take care of him and didn't we do a great thing that time, Dad? Didn't we? Saving his life? Didn't we?

But now I am weeping because we *did* do a great thing that time, even if we were supposed to leave the scraggly little ruffled defiant seabird alone to die and be meat for gulls and crabs. We saved a life, and when you are a little kid and you save the life of a being who would have died without you, you just did the greatest holiest most amazing thing you ever did in your whole life, and the joy and thrill and pride of it goes down into your wild innermost bones, and jazzes you in some sweet mysterious way I don't have words for.

But then we stop saving lives, when we get older. Why?

What Does the Earth Ask of Us?

Mercy. Humility. We thought we were in charge. We took what we could take. And now the subject of the experiment lurches and heaves in rage. Did we think it was not alive, with its own fury to survive? The moral arguments have changed little. The criminal charges have not been filed. No court would accept the brief. And what penalties could be inflicted? We live by symbiosis at best and theft at worst. We are become a parasite on the host that we may well kill, and what will our larvae eat then? The endless empty dark of space?

*

We thought it was a vast farm, from which we could draw fish and deer and corn and petroleum and silver and coal, and the farm had no end; we invented a god to give it to us as a garden of endless delights; but it *does* have an end, it is not infinite, the soil will disappear in sixty years and the fresh water go foul, cities will drown and toddlers die by the millions from diseases that have been waiting ravenously to return and scythe us down like we sliced down the vast seething lungs of the forests. I lived with three toddlers, once. If they had sickened and died from a disease I could trace to its source, to its progenitors, to the casual murderers, I might have been a murderer myself, for all the sheen of civility, all the mask of culture, all my talk of law and order. I might well have been so. Do we abet murder with every gallon of gas we buy, every flight we board? Do we?

*

The ship on which we sail is very much alive; a throbbing machine of parts uncountable and webbed far beyond our science, brilliant as it has grown to be; and the ship asks only one thing of us now, finally, with only this one thing left to ask: that we be creative, and write a novel as big as the world, make a film as endless as the spinning of the earth in the airless void, craft a play with exactly as many parts as there are remaining species of beings left alive, here in the Sixth Extinction. What is the greatest single virtue of our species? What is the one thing that we have in spades and abundance, the one thing that perhaps allowed us to prosper and multiply in such staggering numbers, to send men and machines into the sea of the stars, to fling a chirping robot past the boundaries of our very galaxy? Imagination, brothers and sisters. Imagination. We dream and then make real our dreams. And all that inventiveness, all that innovative zest, all our yearning to solve puzzles and discover secrets and worry inarguable truths from the welter of lies and distractions, all our deep pleasure in making things that were never in the world before in just that way—now that is become the thin thread of our salvation. Not to mention all the other actors in the play. Not to mention your children and their children.

*

Maybe this is why we have attention deficit disorder. Maybe this is why we are mentally fragile and unstable. Maybe this is why we have not been able to corral our violent urges, because somehow imagination is married to anger and fear, and our best dreaming needs desperation or a glimmer of mania as fuel. In which case I suggest we are in an excellent position to dream wildly now, for I am very much afraid that my children, when they are my age, will live in a dark and brooding world where clean air and clean water and clean dirt are only found in photographs and paintings and books and holograms, and religions have sprung up to worship what once was, long ago, before the first of the Water Wars.

*

Maybe we should sue ourselves, for assault and battery, for theft, for rape in the first degree. Do other species have standing in the courts of the human beings? Can osprey testify about their near-death experience, when they were poisoned en masse, and parents were forced to watch as their babies hatched too soon, inside their translucent useless eggshells, and died sobbing for breath, their bones unknit, unable even to mew, unable to see even a shard of the light hatched in the furnaces of the stars? What about trees? Or the thousands and thousands and thousands and thousands and thousands and thousands of kinds of beings slain along the way as we scrabbled for food and money and bigger cars? Or the thousands and thousands of kinds of beings we will never even see or hear or identify or gape at or marvel over who will vanish in their homes in the seething sea, in the misty canopy, in the volcanic vent?

*

We dreamed ourselves aloft. We dreamed ways to wrestle and wrangle rivers. We caught electricity. We persuaded plants to march in rows and give us their children to eat. We dreamed ever faster ways to whir along the skin of the earth in steeds of steel. We dreamed throbbing cities so big and vast and high they seem unreal when we shuffle through them gawking far below. We dreamed the most extraordinary music and the most haunting deep shared stories. We invented uncountable thousands of languages and religions and dances and sports and foods and medicines. Can't we invent new fuels for our steel steeds, and new ways to catch and share energy, and new ways to spin detritus into fuel and energy? Have we gone stale and dim as a species, here at the apex of our population and technology boom? Were these last centuries of incredible invention and innovation and imagination all just for money and power? Or do we have a last slim door through which to send our wild holy imaginations into a future where children do not gasp and retch and duck the bullets of the Water Wars?

Notes

Most of these pieces appeared first in magazines and newspapers, and I thank the discerning editors of *Orion, The Sun, Utne Reader, The American Scholar, Brevity, High Country News, The Indiana Review, Wabash College Magazine, Smokebox, Barnstorm, Our Man in Boston*, and *Ecotone* for their wild belief that their readers would enjoy these inky misadventures. Also my particular thanks to Bronwyn Lattimer, who made me write the long air essay for a stunning National Geographic Society book called *Visions of Paradise* (o man, find it, the photographs will blow your mind), and to Kathleen Dean Moore, who made me write about newts for her and Michael Nelson's glorious book *Moral Ground* (which includes essays by The Dalai Lama and Desmond *Tutu*, for heavenssake). Thanks also to Hannah Fries at *Orion*, who gave the best nature essay ever the chance to be in *Best American Essays 2011*, and to Chip Blake and Hal Clifford at *Orion*, who gave the John Burroughs Association the chance to name the sturgeon essay the best nature essay in America in 2012. That was pretty cool. Chip owes me beer. If a real book from a reputable press says in print that one guy owes another guy beer, it must therefore be so, must it not? My creaky gratitudinous bow also to Cort Conley, whose idea it was to collect all these pieces and who invented the title and wrote the overture, and to Tom Booth, who once again had the mad wit to say *let's do it*, and to Micki Reaman, who edited me gently and courteously when anyone else would shriek and rend his or her garments And finally my love to Mary Miller Doyle, who emitted the three small mammals she and I love best.